# *Dawnlight Breaks*
## The Hymn Texts and Translations of F. Samuel Janzow

David W. Rogner

Lutheran University Press
Minneapolis, Minnesota

Dawnlight Breaks
The Hymn Texts and Translations of F. Samuel Janzow
by David W. Rogner

Copyright © 2014 David W. Rogner. All rights reserved. Published by Lutheran University Press, an imprint of 1517 Media. No part of this book may be reproduced or transmitted in any form by any means, electronic, mechanical, recording, or otherwise, without the express permission of the author. For information or permission for reprints or excerpts, please contact the author.

Published under the auspices of:
Center for Church Music
Concordia University Chicago
River Forest, IL 60305-1402

ISBN-10: 1-942304-00-5

ISBN-13: 978-1-942304-00-5

eISBN: 978-1-942304-51-7

# Contents

Acknowledgements ..................................................................... 5

Introduction ................................................................................ 6

Notes on the Translations:
*The Hymns of Martin Luther* by F. Samuel Janzow ...................... 22

Translations: The Hymns of Martin Luther ................................. 25

Translations of Other German Hymns ......................................... 93

Original Hymn Texts ................................................................. 123

Psalm Paraphrases .................................................................... 159

Notes on the Texts .................................................................... 170

Index of Titles and First Lines ................................................... 193

# Acknowledgments

I am indebted to many people who helped make this volume possible. The first debt is to Dr. Carl Schalk, Distinguished Professor of Music Emeritus at Concordia University Chicago, who encouraged me to deliver a lecture on the hymnody of F. Samuel Janzow at the 2013 Lectures in Church Music Conference at Concordia University Chicago. That year marked the 100th anniversary of Janzow's birth. I am grateful that Dr. Schalk saw me as an appropriate steward of the legacy of Dr. Janzow, who had not only been Dr. Schalk's colleague for many years but who had also, briefly, been my teacher. Dr. Schalk provided me with materials and allowed me to interview him on the life and work of Dr. Janzow.

I am also grateful to Dr. Merle Radke, Distinguished Professor of English Emeritus at Concordia University, who spoke with me at length about his years as Janzow's colleague, providing important biographical details. Dr. Steven Wente, Distinguished Professor of Music at Concordia University, also helped me locate materials and answered numerous musical questions. I am also indebted to my former colleague, the late Dr. Lila Kurth, who spoke with me often over the years about her friendship with Dr. Janzow, all of which helped me to understand the man better. I am also appreciative of the editorial assistance of Barry L. Bobb, Director of the Center for Church Music at Concordia University Chicago, for help in preparing the manuscript.

I am particularly grateful to Christine Janzow Phillips, daughter of Dr. Janzow, for letting me interview her for this project, and also for providing several important academic documents about her father's career as a teacher and writer. She was gracious and supportive throughout the process, helping me understand her father's life and work more clearly.

# Introduction

Dr. F. Samuel Janzow, Professor of English at Concordia—River Forest from 1954 until 1980, produced a remarkable body of hymn texts and translations during his long career. His output includes translations of all 37 of Martin Luther's hymns, as well as translations of dozens of other German hymns. He also composed more than thirty original hymn texts and a number of psalm paraphrases, only a few of which are widely known or currently available in contemporary hymnals. As a member of the LCMS Commission on Worship and member of the Hymn Text and Music committee for *Lutheran Worship* (1982), he played a major role in shaping that hymnal, contributing 28 hymn translations and three original texts. When Dr. Janzow was called to glory in 2001, he left behind a significant contribution to the legacy of Lutheran hymnody. It seems fitting, now that we have recently passed the 100th anniversary of his birth, to collect all of his texts and translations for the first time and to review that contribution. A review of his work is especially interesting in light of the 2006 publication of *Lutheran Service Book,* which chose to use relatively little of his translation work and included only one original text that appeared in *LW.* Consequently, his texts will almost certainly be sung less frequently in Lutheran churches in the coming years. The purpose of this volume is to recognize the great contribution Janzow made to Lutheran hymnody in the twentieth century, to preserve these texts, and to encourage their continued use. This introductory essay provides a brief overview of Janzow's life, examines his hymn-writing career, and analyzes some stylistic features of his texts.

The title of this volume—*Dawnlight Breaks*—is a phrase from one of Janzow's hymn translations: "Comfort, Comfort Says the

Voice." This unusual phrase, in many ways, encapsulates both the theology and the poetry of his hymn-writing. It comes from his translation of Waldemar Rode's "Tröstet, tröstet, spricht der Herr," an Advent hymn based on Isaiah 40. The fourth stanza explores Isaiah's prophecy of John the Baptist, who would prepare the way for the "glory of the Lord," which would be revealed in the Incarnation of Christ. Describing that moment, Janzow writes: "The hour strikes, the dawnlight breaks / God keeps the promises he makes." Poetically, Janzow employs an image not literally found in that particular line of German text. Even more dramatically, he coins the word "dawnlight," a word not found in any dictionary. The image is rooted, however, in the Old Testament prophecy of Jesus as the "sun of righteousness" (Malachi 4:2) and in Jesus' own declaration that he is the "Light of the World" (John 8:12). Theologically, the line typifies Janzow's message as a hymn-writer. The dynamic nature of the Gospel animated his texts, and the Incarnation is that moment in redemptive history when God breaks most dramatically into the world. In all his hymn-writing, however, Janzow wanted the images to match the intensity of the message. Thus a word like "dawnlight" breaks into the poem, offering a poetic flash of illumination, even as it embodies the earth-shaking, life-altering reality of God's love in Jesus Christ.

As a hymn writer, Janzow possessed a fairly unusual pair of credentials: he was an ordained minister of the Lutheran Church—Missouri Synod who also had a Ph.D. in literary studies. These two credentials actually combine to help explain the nature of his literary output. As a Lutheran pastor, he was devoted to writing texts that were faithful to Scripture and the Lutheran confessions, filled with a clear expression of Law and Gospel. But the form of these texts reflects his immersion in the formal study of literature. Janzow's graduate study of literature, culminating in a Ph.D. in English from the University of Chicago in 1968, occurred at a time when formalism (or the New Criticism) was at its height. Formalism emphasized the "organic wholeness" of a poem. It argued that a poem should balance discordant qualities and ultimately produce a coherent whole, in which all the parts contribute to the overall effect. Janzow's texts often illustrate this maxim, as he strives to makes every detail correspond to his overall theme. Formalism also paid attention to devices like alliteration and assonance, and Janzow's texts are filled with examples that show how he chose words carefully for the way they sounded.

But in addition to being a literary scholar, Dr. Janzow was also a pastor. He was, first of all, the son of a Lutheran pastor. Born Bertram Frederick Samuel Janzow in 1913 in Calgary, Alberta, Canada, where his father was serving a Lutheran congregation, he grew up mostly in Minnesota and attended Concordia—St. Paul, Minnesota, for high school and junior college. After graduating from Concordia Seminary, St. Louis, in 1936, he received a call that resulted in perhaps the most formative experience of his life. He was called to serve as assistant pastor of Luther-Tyndale Church in London, England. Three years later his fiancée, Lydia Marie Pieper, came to England, and they were married in London just as the Second World War was breaking out. To make matters worse, the senior pastor—a native German—returned to visit Germany just before Hitler's invasion of Poland and was not allowed to return to England. Janzow was left—as a young pastor and a newlywed—to shepherd the congregation by himself through the London blitz, as German bombers conducted nightly air-raids on the city. Merle Radke, his long-time friend and colleague from the English Department, said that, although Janzow was reluctant to discuss it, he would occasionally talk to him about the "sheer terror of those London days." Janzow remained in London through the entire war, returning to the United States in 1947 after 11 years at Luther-Tyndale.

The London experiences, however, appear to have never left him completely. We see evidence of this in a poem by his colleague Karl Sorenson, written to honor Janzow on the occasion of his retirement. In this poem, "A Retracing," published in *Motif* in 1984, Sorenson paints a picture of Janzow during the London years, depicting him as "an air-warden, attempting to outwit the V-2 maze without, the silent wounds within." When Janzow wrote or translated texts describing how "roaring devils fill the world" or "floods of evil threaten," he spoke from a place he understood emotionally. Those experiences also convinced him, however, of God's grace and divine protection. He was grateful for God's rescue of body and soul. Janzow suffered with health issues throughout his life, and Merle Radke believes that Janzow sometimes produced hymn texts in grateful response to moments of healing and recovery. When the storm clouds of ill health receded, Janzow would use his poetic gifts to give thanks to God.

When Janzow returned to America, he first completed a master's degree in English at the University of Minnesota, at which time he took a call back to a parish in Trimont, Minnesota. After six years at that parish, he received a call in 1954 to teach theology and English at Concordia Teachers College, River Forest. Fourteen years later he received his Ph.D. from the University of Chicago, after completing a dissertation on the British author Thomas DeQuincey. His research was a painstaking, scholarly analysis of unsigned pieces of journalism in British newspapers. Janzow worked to attribute these to DeQuincey, based largely on stylistic analysis. When British publishers Pickering and Chatto produced their 21-volume *Works of Thomas DeQuincey* (2002), they included the pieces that Janzow had attributed to DeQuincey, foot-noting his research on numerous occasions as having contributed to their eventual attribution.

In addition to his scholarship on Dequincey, Janzow produced some other significant translation work during his career. His translation of *Luther's Large Catechism: A Contemporary Translation with Study Questions* was published in 1978 by Concordia Publishing House. He also prepared a translation of Johann Walter's *Lob und Preis der löblichen Kunst Musica* ("In Praise of the Noble Art of Music"), a didactic poem written in 1538 in which Walter developed an entire theology of music based on Luther's views.

Merle Radke, in describing Janzow, said he was "happiest being a scholar," whether that meant conducting literary research or translating Luther's hymns. Even those who knew him best, however, confess to knowing little about this rather private man—or about his process as a writer. Radke described Janzow as "a bashful man who underestimated his own worth." In the aforementioned poem honoring Janzow's retirement, Karl Sorenson described him as "a gentle man, promptly polite" and as one with "self-effacing formal easiness" and "shy dignity." Carl Schalk set many of Janzow's texts to music, but Schalk claims to know little of Janzow's process, saying that they never really "collaborated." Janzow produced texts independently, which he gave to Schalk in completed form. He seems to have produced the majority of his hymns and translations when other people asked him to do so. Schalk, for example, encouraged Janzow to translate all of Luther's hymns. He claims that Janzow, although he had already translated several of them, produced the rest of the work in a remarkably short period of time. This claim is supported by an academic document obtained from the Janzow family entitled "Summer Activities, 1970, of F. Samuel Janzow," in which he lists 27 hymns of Luther, apparently translated over the course of a summer. Despite this prodigious output and his zealous dedication to the task, Janzow was the epitome of humble service, always reluctant to put himself forward or promote his work.

Colleagues and family members have provided a few other hints about Janzow's work habits. His daughter, Christine Janzow Phillips, remembers her parents sitting together at the piano at home, with Lydia playing the tune so Sam could sing his text and test how it fit the tune. Radke stated that Janzow would bring drafts of hymn texts to the daily English Department "coffee break" and pass them around to colleagues for reactions. Henry Lettermann, in fact, recounts these occasions in his own poem honoring Janzow ("Tribute," *Motif*, 1984), in which he remembers "the earnest afternoon's impromptu hymn-sings." Both Janzow and Lettermann tried their hymns out on their department colleagues, especially in the years they were working on the hymnody for *Lutheran Worship*. Often, Radke said, Janzow would inquire whether particular words seemed too antiquarian or obscure. He was concerned that sometimes he reached too far in looking for a good, poetic image. One of Janzow's other contributions to Concordia–River Forest was his establishment of an annual literary magazine there—known as *Motif*—which he began in 1960. Many of Janzow's and Lettermann's texts first appeared in *Motif*, which he edited (along with Lettermann) for the remainder of his career. This provided a "testing ground" for a number of his hymns, some of which were published there in new settings by colleagues from the Concordia music department.

It is difficult to know exactly when—and under what circumstances—Janzow first began to write hymn texts and translations. His first published text, however, appears to be one of the ones for which he is best known—and arguably one of his best: "From Shepherding of Stars." When it first appeared in *Lutheran Education* in 1963, with a tune by Richard Hillert, Janzow was already 50 years old. His most prolific period, however, was between 1969 and 1982. Throughout the late 1960s and early 1970s, he most commonly wrote translations and original texts when asked to do so by his colleagues. Original texts like "Gabriel, You Brought to Mary" were written for *Lutheran Education* (at the urging of Merle Radke, its editor), and Janzow published German translations both in *Motif* and in the journal *Church Music*, encouraged by colleagues in the music department, who wrote new settings for his translations. His first publications in a Lutheran hymnal were three texts that appeared in *Worship Supplement* in 1969: the original text "From Shepherding of Stars" and two translations: "We Praise, O Christ, Your Holy Name" and "Let All Together Praise Our God."

The complete collection of Luther's hymns, encouraged by Schalk, was published on the Concordia campus in 1976. The new translations appeared in settings by Paul Bunjes, Richard Hillert, and Carl Schalk, usually for some combination of choir, congregation, and instruments. Between 1978 and 1982, these new translations and settings were published in six volumes by Concordia Publishing House. Ten of these Martin Luther hymn translations—in one form or another—were included in *Lutheran Worship* in 1982. An even greater contribution to *Lutheran Worship*, however, came in the form of 18 other German hymn translations, by writers such as Paul Gerhardt, Johann Walter, Nikolaus Herman, and Valentin Thilo.

Another collaborative project of the early 1970s was the publication by Janzow, Carl Schalk, and Paul Bunjes of a volume called *Psalms for the Church Year for Congregation and Choir*, published in 1975 by Augsburg Publishing House. This volume included eleven psalms, as well as paraphrases of *The Venite, The Magnificat,* and a *Phos hilaron* (which was incorporated into a setting of the *Nunc Dimittis*.) These psalms were designed to be sung by alternating between chanted verses of the psalm and metrical paraphrases of psalm verses, written by Janzow. According to the volume's preface, the metrical paraphrases were designed to "restate in more contemporary language the content of the prose verses chanted previously" or to "reflect on the content of the psalm text just heard." This volume includes the metrical psalm paraphrases as stand-alone texts, leaving out the prose verses of each psalm. (Three of those psalm paraphrases—67, 128, and 130—were translations of Luther's versions of the psalms and so appear in this volume with the other Luther translations.)

The final years of Janzow's teaching career—the late 1970s—were dominated by his work on the Hymn Text and Music Committee for *Lutheran Worship*, to which he was appointed in 1978. In the period after *Lutheran Worship* was published, Janzow turned his attention away from translations and toward a new project involving original texts. He began writing texts to be used in worship on days commemorating saints or on other "lesser" festivals. This resulted in the publication of a 38-page booklet in 1983 called *Sing Glorias for All His Saints* (CPH). This text-only publication (which includes suggestions for tunes) appears to have been designed for daily chapel worship at the college, where minor festivals are more regularly observed. In the introductory notes, Janzow observes: "As awareness of the church's liturgical heritage grows, parish observance of the saints' days are likely to increase." Fully aware that these festivals only occasionally fall on Sundays, he discourages any "rigid notions of the fixity of a given festival's calendar date." He rather encourages Christians to consider them "moveable feast[s]" and celebrate them on Sundays, thereby allowing these hymns to be used more widely. Most of these texts are relatively unknown. However, one of them—"Praise God for John, Evangelist"—was included in *The Hymnal 1982* of the Episcopal Church. Many of these deserve to be more widely used in Christian churches of all denominations.

The chart on pages 18 and 19 lists the inclusion of Janzow texts in four Lutheran hymnals: *Worship Supplement, Lutheran Book of Worship, Lutheran Worship,* and *Lutheran Service Book.* The translations section identifies with a + those texts that first appeared in *The Hymns of Martin Luther,* before being printed in *Lutheran Worship*. In some case, however, those texts have even earlier incarnations, which are described in the notes on the hymns at the end of the volume. The chart offers a "snapshot" of how Janzow's hymnody came into use in Lutheran worship in the late twentieth-century. *Lutheran Worship* contains by far the greatest number of his texts. As the right-hand column indicates, the 2006 *Lutheran Service Book* moved toward "composite translation" of German hymns, using bits and pieces of Janzow's translations but not including a single whole translation from *LW*. Only one of his original texts appears in *LSB*: "Lord, When You Came as Welcome Guest," a text Janzow composed for the occasion of his son's wedding.

Janzow's style, as noted above, emphasizes fresh, original language and the clustering of images around a central theme. His texts speak Gospel truths by using Biblical imagery, but typically he amplifies or extends this imagery, carrying it throughout a text to create a sense of coherence. Sometimes he creates brand new images or metaphors to communicate the Gospel, and here readers may differ on how successfully he accomplishes his objectives. Perhaps Janzow's Christmas carol "From Shepherding of Stars" best illustrates his original use of language. It also shows his devotion to unifying the stanzas of a hymn by repeating and extending the central metaphor. The entire hymn is spoken by the angel who announces the birth of Jesus to shepherds. The opening lines depict the angel as one who has come "from shepherding of stars that gaze / Toward heav'nly fields of light." Having begun with this unusual image of the angel as a *shepherd of stars*, Janzow depicts the angel *coming to shepherds* so that he might tell them of a newborn King who is Himself a *Shepherd*. In the sonically and theologically rich fourth stanzas, the angel says of Jesus: "He shepherds from the thistled place / The flocks by thickets torn; / His piercéd hands heal all your race / Sore wounded by the thorn." Here Janzow prefigures the nails that will pierce the Good Shepherd's hands, even as he alludes to the thistles and thickets that, since the Fall, have torn and wounded the sheep. The newborn Christ, however, has come to heal these wounds. The poem unites all of the images in the final stanza when the narrator urges: "To shepherd-healer-king let throngs / Sing glorias again."

Janzow also creates a striking sense of formal unity in his translation of Luther's *Was fürchtst du, Fiend Herodes sehr,* which he entitles "Why Would Foe Herod and His Horde." The first line, to begin with, plays cleverly on Herod's name by using the word "horde," which is an anagram for Herod. Janzow's earlier draft of the hymn had been called "Why Does Foe Herod and His Horde," but—by changing the first words to "Why would"—he heightened the alliteration, both with the initial "w" sounds and the final "d" sounds. He describes the wise men as coming with a "three-fold noble gift" and then proceeds to create a series of "threes" to expand this imagery. He states that the magi's gifts declare Jesus to be "God, man, and king." In stanza three, concerning Christ's baptism, he identifies three things that the Savior will do: "take our place, / Wash sin away, and give us grace." In the final stanza, he refers to Jesus as "Lord, Christ, and King," before ending with a Trinitarian "Father, Holy Ghost, and He." In a poetic fourth stanza, Janzow uses some brilliant parallelism and alliteration.

> The Living Word at Cana spoke
> And water into wine awoke.
> His Gospel word wakes hearts of men
> To serve God's purposes again.

The five "w" sounds in the two internal lines are an effective use of alliteration, and he sets up a fascinating parallel between two kinds of "waking" by declaring that the water "awoke" into wine in the working of that miracle. Assisted by the alliterative "w's," he can then compare that "waking" with how the Gospel message "wakes" human hearts.

Janzow's penchant for thematic unity can also be seen in "The Very Skies Served You, O Lord," his Maundy Thursday hymn about Christ washing of the disciples' feet. Here he writes a five-stanza text united by the images of cleansing. He depicts Christ as humbly washing feet, despite the fact that the "very skies" (which drop cleansing rain) are obedient to Him. In stanzas 2-3, Christ's literal foot-washing is then connected to how Christ came as servant to "cleanse us from iniquity" and wash us "in mercy's boundless sea." The fourth stanza acknowledges that "sin's grime keeps collecting still" and calls upon the Lord to "gird yourself anew / To wash us and renew our will." The final stanza depicts us as "refreshed" by this washing so that we might bend down in service (as Jesus did in the first stanza) to serve "the Lazarus at the gate."

One final example of his repetition and thematic unity can be found in a text written for the festival of The Presentation: "In Her Arms the Blessed Virgin." The hymn opens with a picture of the Virgin carrying the infant Christ to the temple for his presentation. Each of the four stanzas then extends the idea of "carrying, "holding," or "bearing." In the second stanza we are encouraged to "cradle in our hearts this infant." The third stanza begins with the admonition: "May our Simeon-faith hold Jesus." The fourth stanza ends with the prayer: "Strong be our faith's hold to cherish / This our Ransom, source of grace, / In the deep heart's core enfolding / Him who won us God's embrace." Here we are asked to "hold" the Infant by our faith and to "enfold" him in the "deep heart's core" (a phrase which seems to make a literary allusion to W. B. Yeats's poem "The Lake Isle of Innisfree," which ends "I hear it in the deep heart's core.")

Janzow's hymns are also rich in organic metaphors. He frequently uses Scripture's own images of God's word as seed and of the Christian life (and the Kingdom of God) as a plant that grows and must be nourished. In "You Planted Us in Sun and Rain," a hymn he says is for "Assignment to Ministry," he depicts Christian workers who have been "planted . . . in sun and rain" as now ready to be "transplanted . . . to what field you will" in order to "bear your Holy Spirit's fruits." In another original text called "Thy Planting," he uses "vine and branches" images to depict the organic growth of a Christian life. He first asks that Christ might "Baptismal faith seed in / With thorn-pierced hand." In the final stanza, he prays that the cross might be a canopy against the storm "Till heaven prolong / The vineyard song / Of branches raised to share / Thy victory." In a baptismal hymn entitled "Great God, You Gave a Gleaming Earth," he describes how we were "dead clay" before our baptism, after which our hearts, once an "arid plain," can "bloom" when God sends rain—a life that "toward glory grows." All of these examples illustrate how devoted he was to depicting the Christian life as a living, growing entity, begun in baptism and leading to everlasting life.

What one must admit, however, about Janzow's fresh and striking imagery, is that it sometimes produced texts that are difficult or jarring. The "poetic" Janzow, in other words, could make a singing congregation uncomfortable. While many of his texts, of course, do work beautifully as sung texts, others "read" better as poems than they "sing." This may help explain why the *LSB* editors passed over much of his work. A few examples will illustrate this point. For instance, in his translation of "O People, Rise and Labor" (*LW* 25), an Advent hymn that invites us to prepare for the Lord and make straight His path, he declares that we should "The sunken valleys fill / Restore eroded places / Where sinbursts leave their traces." While "sinburst" is certainly a clever play on—and reversal of—the word "sunburst," the novelty of it may sound more distracting than worshipful. In his translation of "Christ with Death the Battle Fought," he depicts Christ as going "into no-man's-land," an image that more likely conjures up the battlefields of World War I, rather than Christ's battle against Satan. In his translation "If God Were Not Beside Us Now," as he describes the enemies of God, he uses a jarring image that may offend by its rawness: "Thanks be to God, who did not let / Their eager jawbones snatch us." The "eager jawbones," while they conjure a vivid picture of the enemy, may seem indecorous in the worship setting. These exemplify Janzow's tendency to sometimes "reach too far" and thus produce words or phrases that congregations are uncomfortable singing.

Despite these shortcomings, Janzow's texts are often powerful and always theologically astute. His translations remain a remarkable achievement, especially in terms of their breadth and scope. Equally important are his original texts, many of which remain unknown and deserve to be more widely used in worship. His original texts for saint days and minor festivals provide a valuable resource for worship planners. This volume would serve a worthy purpose if it inspired contemporary composers to set some of these deserving texts to music.

A few texts should be called out here for special attention. One of Janzow's most beautiful texts in *Lutheran Worship* is "Jesus, Shepherd in Your Arms," a translation of Johann Meinhold's hymn for the occasion of the death and funeral of a child. Although congregations have limited use for such a hymn, Janzow created a text with beautiful pastoral imagery in which the sick child is cradled in the hands of the loving Shepherd and taken to a place with "meadows only fair" and where the young lamb "Has its sighs all turned to singing." Paired in *LW* with a tune that seems incongruous, the text deserves a new, more appropriate tune. His little-known hymn "We Praise Your Call to Matthew" skillfully employs images of wealth to depict how this money-driven tax-collector traded his "book-keeping pen" for the pen of a Gospel writer. Suitable not only for St. Matthew's day, the hymn encourages all Christians to make their material goods "wholly dedicated, Lord Jesus, to Your will." The hymn "You Planted Us in Sun and Rain" (which Janzow said was for "Assignment to Ministry") could be profitably used in Christian graduations and commissioning services; the hymn depicts Christians being "transplanted" in other fields where they might "bear Your Holy Spirit's fruits." Finally, his wedding text, "Lord, When You Came as Welcome Guest" (*LSB* 859; *LW* 252), provides a beautiful prayer for a Christian wedding. It begins with Christ's blessing of the wedding at Cana by his presence, continues by comparing the couple's bond to the marriage of Christ and His Church, and then includes this beautiful prayer: "Your daily mercies let them share, / All threats of harm destroy; / By this their vow divide their care / And double all their joy." Although this text appears to be heavily indebted to "Lord, Who at Cana's Wedding-Feast," an earlier hymn by Adelaide Thrupp (stanzas 1 and 3) and Godfrey Thring (stanza 2), Janzow recasts it in fresh language that faithfully depicts Christian marriage, offering godly encouragement to the bridal couple. In it we see—as is almost always the case in Janzow's texts—both the pastor and the poet at work.

His dual commitment to theology and poetry can be seen in a comment he made in 1992 in an article that appeared in *Lutheran Worship Notes*. Responding to a question about the principles of hymn selection for *Lutheran Worship* (ten years after the hymnal's publication) Janzow noted: "The operative criteria were such as would be expected of an LCMS Commission on Worship aware of its responsibility: hymn content in harmony with Scripture; appropriateness for Lutheran liturgical public worship; excellence of poetic form and content in terms of unity of construction; usability by all sharers of the Apostolic faith." The emphasis he places here on both Scriptural faithfulness and poetic excellence reflects the principles that animated his own hymn writing, in which the poet and the pastor worked together to craft beautiful expressions of the grace of God.

## HYMN TEXTS OF F. SAMUEL JANZOW

in *Worship Supplement* (WS), *Lutheran Book of Worship* (LBW), *Lutheran Worship* (LW), and *Lutheran Service Book* (LSB).

### Original Texts

| | | | |
|---|---|---|---|
| "From Shepherding of Stars" | WS 713 | | |
| "Look Toward the Mountains" | | | LW 71 |
| | | | LW 310 |
| "Lord, When You Came as Welcome Guest" | | | LW 252 / LSB 859 |

### Translations

| | | |
|---|---|---|
| "Christ Is Arisen" | LW 124 | |
| "'Comfort, Comfort,' Says the Voice" | LW 21 | |
| "Entrust Your Days and Burdens" | LW 427 | LSB 754* |
| "From Depths of Woe I Cry to You" (alt.) | LW 230 | |
| "From Heaven Came the Angel Bright" + (alt.) | LW 52 | |
| "God Brought Me to This Time and Place" | LW 456 | |
| "Grant, Holy Ghost, that We Behold" | LW 336 | |
| "Grant, Lord Jesus, that My Healing" | LW 95 | |
| "Here Is the Tenfold Sure Command" + | LW 331 | LSB 581* |
| "In Peace and Joy I Now Depart" + | LW 185 | LSB 938* |
| "In the Very Midst of Life" + | LW 265 | |
| "Isaiah, Mighty Seer, in Spirit Soared" + (alt.) | LW 214 | |

| | | | |
|---|---|---|---|
| "Jesus Christ, Our Blessed Savior" # | | LW 236/37 | LSB 627* |
| "Jesus, Shepherd, in Your Arms" | | LW 269 | |
| "Let All Together Praise Our God" | | LW 44 | LSB 389* |
| "Lift Up Your Heads, You Might Gates" | | LW 23/24 | |
| "Lord Jesus Christ, Will You Not Stay" | WS 712 | LW 344 | LSB 585* |
| "May God Embrace Us with His Grace" + (alt.) | | LW 288 | |
| "Now Let Us Come Before Him" | | LW 184 | |
| "Now Sing We, Now Rejoice" | | LW 47 | LBW 47 |
| "O People, Rise and Labor" | | LW 25 | |
| "O Darkest Woe" | | LW 122* | |
| "Our Father, Who from Heaven Above" + (alt.) | | LW 431 | LSB 766* |
| "Savior of the Nations, Come" + (alt.) | | LW 13 | LSB 332* |
| "The Bridegroom Soon Will Call Us" | | LW 176 | LSB 514* |
| "We All Believe in One True God, Maker" + | | LW 213 | |
| "We Praise, O Christ, Your Holy Name" + # | WS 708 | LW 35 | |
| "When I Suffer Pains and Losses" | | LW 423 | |

+ printed in *The Hymns of Martin Luther* at Concordia–River Forest 1976; published in six volumes by CPH, 1978-82

# published earlier in *Church Music*

* includes only a portion of the original translation

Introduction | 19

## EDITORIAL PRACTICE

The texts that follow are organized into four sections. First are Janzow's translations of the hymns of Martin Luther. These are followed by his translations of other German hymns. The third section contains all of Janzow's original hymn texts, and the fourth section contains his psalm paraphrases.

The primary copy-text for most of the hymns of Martin Luther is the six-volume *The Hymns of Martin Luther*, published by Concordia Publishing House between 1978 and 1982. When any of these texts was published earlier, in identical or only slightly-altered versions, these other publications and variants are indicated in the notes. *Lutheran Worship* (1982) provides the copy text for those translations of Luther's hymns in which Janzow himself appears to have altered what he published earlier in *The Hymns of Martin Luther*. If *LW* attributed the translation to Janzow but indicated (with the abbreviation "alt.") that it was altered by the *LW* editors, then Janzow's earlier, original text is used as the copy-text.

In cases where Janzow published substantially different translations—over time—of the same text, the multiple versions are included. Janzow, for instance, published three substantially different translations of "A Mighty Fortress Is Our God" (in 1970, 1975, and 1983), all of which are included for comparison. Multiple versions of some other non-Luther translations are also included. Notable among these are Johann Walter's "The Bridegroom Soon Will Call Us" (*LW 176*) and an earlier version, "The Bridegroom's Voice Will Soon Be Heard," as well as Valentin Thilo's "O People, Rise and Labor" (*LW 25*) and an earlier version, "All People, Now Make Ready." For most of Janzow's translations of non-Luther hymns, the *Lutheran Worship* text serves as the copy text.

*Sing Glorias for All His Saints* (1983) serves as the copy-text for twenty-four original hymns; one text published there —"Great God, You Drew a Gleaming Earth"—was slightly revised for *Motif* in 1984, which serves as the copy-text. Beneath the title of each of these hymns is the name of the festival or occasion (provided by Janzow) for which the hymn was written. Several hymns appeared only in *Motif* (published by Concordia-River Forest) or in the journal *Church Music* (published by CPH and edited by the Concordia-River Forest faculty from 1966 to 1980), in which cases these journals serve as the source.

# Notes on the Translations
## The Hymns of Martin Luther (1978-82)

### by F. Samuel Janzow

These translations of Luther's thirty-seven hymns are committed neither to the academic tradition of strict translation nor to the tradition of free re-creation. While the former aims at complete semantic accuracy, the latter strives for a reincarnation of the inner spirit of the original. In poetry, free re-creation is almost mandatory, but it involves frequent sacrifice of the original semantic and syntactic patterns. In the present work, any ambition to exploit this method was restricted by requirements of the prosody. For example, since the hymns of Luther were assumed to be inseparably wedded to their melodies, the meter was not open to choice, and the frequent feminine rhymes—much less graceful in English than in German—had to be retained.

Another consideration was the fact that Luther's hymns are less an expression of subjective emotion than a confession and proclamation of basic teachings of the Christian faith. Capturing the inner spirit of Luther's hymns therefore required above all else a faithful representation of Luther's Biblical faith. Nevertheless, the translator felt free to handle Luther's subordinate ideas and imagery with considerable freedom. One will therefore find transpositions of order, paraphrased expressions in place of literal reproductions, the selection of certain values in a given poetic image to the necessary neglect of some others, and sometimes even the substitution of entirely different images. In no instance, however, was it the intention to alter the Biblical and Reformation concepts in Luther's hymns. The church delights to be captive to the Word also in its hymnody.

The German texts of Luther's hymns are readily available. His translation into German of the *Gloria in Excelsis (All' Ehr und Lob soll Gottes sein)* is in Konrad Ameln, *et al.*, eds., *Handbuch der deutschen evangelischen Kirchenmusik*, I, 572. His "German Sanctus," (*Jesaia, dem Propheten, das geschah*) is from the *Deudsche Messe und ordnung Gottis diensts*, which is in *D. Martin Luthers Werke, Kritische Gesamtausgabe* (Weimar: 1883), XIX, 72-113. The remaining hymns are found in the same edition, Vol. XXXV, pp. 411-497.

# TRANSLATIONS: THE HYMNS OF MARTIN LUTHER

# *A Mighty Fortress Is Our God (I)*
[*Ein feste Burg ist unser Gott*]

A mighty Fortress is our God
    Strong Shield and sturdy Weapon,
Rock of defense and smiting Rod
    When hordes of evil threaten.
Still fierce, our ancient foe
Wants only our woe,
Comes armed with brute might,
Deceit and deadly spite.
    In God alone is rescue.

To trust in our vain human might
    Would forge our quick surrender.
One Man wrings vict'ry from the fight,
    By God's choice our Defender.
You ask me for His name?
Christ Jesus, the same
Who reigns on God's throne,
Lord Sabaoth alone.
    He holds the field in triumph.

Though demons' roaring fills the world
    Intent on our damnation,
We scorn our fear and raise unfurled
    The banner of salvation.
The prince of darkness scowls,
Unceasingly prowls.
Fear not! His doom's sealed,
For God Himself revealed
    The simple Word that fells him.

That Word, despite all foes, will stand,
    And let them always hear it!
The Word stands by us, His strong hand
    Supplies His gifts and Spirit.
And if foes take by strife
Goods, fame, kindred, life,
Then such be our loss,
For we still keep the cross,
    We hold the crown and kingdom.

*Copyright © 1970 Concordia Publishing House*

# A Mighty Fortress Is Our God (II)
[*Ein feste Burg ist unser Gott*]

A mighty fortress is our God,
Our stronghold and our weapon.
He shields us when affliction's rod
And floods of evil threaten.
Still fierce, our ancient Foe,
All out to work woe,
Comes armed with great might,
Deep cunning, deadly spite.
God's grace is our one refuge.

To trust in our own human might
Would forge our quick surrender.
God sends His Man into the fight
To be our great defender.
You do not know His name?
Christ Jesus, the same
Who reigns on God's throne,
Our Lord, He strives alone
And holds the field, triumphant.

Though roaring devils fill the world
To drive us to the burning,
The banner of the Lamb unfurled
Shows how the battle's turning.
Their Prince may darkly rage,
His legions engage—
God's crucified arm
Struck down his pow'r to harm.
One Word, our Christ, can fell him.

The Word of God shall stand secure
Though millions flout and jeer it.
Our Christ is with us to ensure
Our power in the Spirit.

And though they take our life,
Goods, fame, child, and wife,
For them shines no sun,
Our victory is won,
We keep cross, crown, and kingdom.

*Copyright © 1975 Concordia Publishing House*

# A Mighty Fortress Is Our God (III)
[*Ein feste Burg ist unser Gott*]

A mighty fortress is our God,
A shield and glorious weapon.
He frees us from the tyrant rod
Of evils that now threaten.
Our old most wicked foe,
Who swears to work woe,
Comes armed with dread spite,
Deep cunning, deadly might,
And none but God can quell him.

We have no strength to match his might.
We soon would fall, rejected;
But see, the right man joins our fight,
The champion God selected.
"Who is he?" you may ask.
Christ takes on our task;
God's Son, the one Lord
By angel hosts adored,
Will hold the field, and triumph.

Though devil legions fill the world
To drive us to the burning,
Christ's banner joyfully unfurled
Shows how the battle's turning.
Their prince may scowl and rage,
His forces engage,
Yet we escape harm:
God's judgment binds his arm!
One little word can fell him.

God's Word stands firm amid the fray;
In vain men spurn and jeer it.
God's at our side, we win the day
With weapons of his Spirit.

Though they may harm our life,
Goods, fame, child, and wife,
The victory Christ won
Can never be undone.
We hold cross, crown, and kingdom!

*Copyright © F. Samuel Janzow*

# A New Song Now Shall Be Begun

[*Ein neues Lied wir haben an*]

A new song now shall be begun,
Lord, help us raise the banner
Of praise for all that God has done,
For which we give Him honor.
At Brussels in the Netherlands
God proved Himself most truthful
And poured His gifts from open hands
On two lads, martyrs youthful,
Through whom He showed His power.

One was named John, a name to show
He stood in God's high favor.
His brother Henry, well we know,
Was salt of truest savor.
This world they now have left behind
And wear bright crowns of glory.
These sons of God had fixed the mind
Upon the Gospel story,
For which they died as martyrs.

From where the foe in ambush lay,
He sent to have them taken
To force them God's Word to betray
And make their faith be shaken.
Louvain sent clever men, who came
In twisting nets to break them.
Hard played they at their crooked game,
But from faith could not shake them.
God made their tricks look foolish.

Oh, they sang sweet, and they sang sour,
They tried all their devices.
The youths stood firmly like a tow'r
And overcame each crisis.

It filled the Foe with raging hate
To show himself defeated
By these two lads, and he so great.
His rage flared high, and heated
His plan to see them burning.

Their cloister-garments off they tore,
Took off their consecrations;
All this the youths were ready for,
They said Amen with patience.
They gave to God the Father thanks
That He would them deliver
From Satan's scoffing and the pranks
That make men quake and shiver
When he comes masked and raging.

The God they worshipped granted them
A priesthood in Christ's order.
They offered up themselves to Him
And crossed His kingdom's border
By dying to the world outright,
With ev'ry falsehood breaking.
They came to heaven, pure and white;
All monkery forsaking,
They turned away from evil.

A paper given them to sign—
And carefully they read it—
Spelled out their faith in ev'ry line
As they confessed and said it.
Their greatest fault was to be wise
And say, "We trust God solely,
For human wisdom is all lies,
We should distrust it wholly."
This brought them to the burning.

Then two great fires were set alight,

While men amazed did ponder
The sight of youths who showed no fright;
Their calm filled men with wonder.
They stepped into the flames with song,
God's grace and glory praising.
The logic choppers puzzled long
But found these new things dazing
Which God was here displaying.

They now regret their deed of shame,
Would like to slough it over;
They dare not glory in their blame,
But put it under cover.
They feel their gnawing infamy,
Their friends hear them deplore it.
God's Spirit cannot silent be,
But on Cain's guilty forehead
He marks the blood of Abel.

The ashes of the lads remain
And scatter to all places.
They rise from roadway, street, and lane
To mark the guilty faces.
The Foe has used a bloody hand
To keep these voices quiet,
But they resist in ev'ry land
The Foe's rage and defy it.
The ashes go on singing.

And yet men still keep up their lies
To justify the killing;
The Foe with falsehood ever tries
To give to guilt clean billing.
Since these young martyrs' holy death
Men still continue trying
To say, the youths with their last breath
Renounced their faith when dying
And finally recanted.

Let men heap falsehoods all around,
Their sure defeat is spawning.
We thank our God the Word is found,
We stand in its bright dawning.
Our summer now is at the door,
The winter's frost has ended,
Soft bud the flowers more and more,
By our dear Gard'ner tended
Until He reaps His harvest.

*Copyright © 1982 Concordia Publishing House*

*[This folk ballad was probably Luther's first hymn. It was written to commemorate the heroic faith of the first two martyrs of the Reformation: Heinrich Voes and Johann Esch.]*

## *All Glory Be to God Alone*
[*All Ehr und Lob soll Gottes sein*]

All glory be to God alone,
Supreme upon the highest throne.
He made His wrath toward men to cease,
Bends down to us in grace and peace.
May mankind welcome His good will,
May thankfulness their singing fill.

Lord God, we bless Your holy name
With praise ascending like a flame.
Your awesome majesty we feel,
Toward Your eternal glory kneel,
Adoring You by day and night
As our great source of life and light.

King reigning in the heav'ns above,
Our mighty Father, God of love,
And You who from the Father came,
Now bearing God's eternal name,
Christ, Son of God, eternal Lamb,
You are our Lord, the great I Am.

You took the whole world's sin away;
Have mercy on us, Lord, we pray.
You took the whole world's sin away;
Give ear, O Lord, to what we pray.
Enthroned in God's eternal day,
Shine mercy on us, Lord, we pray.

You are the ever-holy One;
Lord, You rule all things, You alone.
You as the only Lord most high,
Dear Savior, Christ, we glorify.
The Father's equal on the throne,
You are with God the Spirit one.

Amen, this is forever true.
The angel throngs confess it, too.
The world You made joins in the praise
That echoes through eternal days.
All Christendom will ever raise
To Your great glory endless praise.

*Copyright © 1979 Concordia Publishing House*

# All the Nations' Savior, Come
[*Nun komm, der Heiden Heiland*]

All the nations' Savior, come,
Show Yourself the Virgin's Son.
Marvel, heaven, wonder, earth,
That our Lord chose such a birth.

No man's pow'r of mind or blood,
But the Spirit of our God
Made the Word of God be flesh,
Woman's offspring, pure and fresh.

Here a maid was found with child,
Virgin pure and undefiled.
By her virtues it was known
God has made her heart His throne.

Then stepped forth the Lord of all
From His pure and kingly hall;
God of God, becoming man,
His heroic course began.

God the Father was his source,
Back to God He ran His course.
Into hell His road went down,
Back then to His throne and crown.

Father's Equal, You will win
Vict'ries in us over sin.
Might Eternal, make us whole;
Heal our ills of flesh and soul.

From the manger newborn light
Sends a glory through the night.
Night cannot this light subdue.
Faith keeps springing ever new.

Glory to the Father sing,
Glory to the Son, our King,
Glory to the Spirit be
Now and through eternity.

*Copyright © 1978 Concordia Publishing House*

# Christ Jesus to the Jordan Came

[*Christ unser Herr zum Jordan kam*]

Christ Jesus to the Jordan came
To be baptized like others,
Our Lord and Brother without blame
As Stand-in for His brothers.
A new baptismal tide He gave,
To wash away sin's mountain
And drown the pow'r of death and grave,
His cross and wounds the fountain
Of new life for believers.

So listen now and do note well
God's sacramental action
And what we must believe and tell
To overcome all faction.
We use plain water, as God wills;
Faith comes to life that hour,
For Gospel Word that water fills
With all the Spirit's power.
It's He that does the washing.

God placed this truth before our eyes
There at the Jordan River.
From heaven came, to men's surprise,
The word that echoes ever
In hearts that trust what God has done:
"This Jesus is my Pleasure;
This Man is my beloved Son
And your own greatest Treasure.
Hear Him and do His bidding."

We see the God-man Jesus stand
Beneath the op'ning heaven;
The Spirit, dove-formed by God's hand,
To His dear Son is given.

Let not a doubt in us arise
That in our holy washing
Our God himself came to baptize
And pour on us His blessing
That He might live within us.

Christ bids His loyal friends to tell
The world its lost condition,
How sin dooms it to deepest hell
Unless it learns contrition.
But he who trusts and is baptized
Will never, never perish;
Instead, by joy and life surprised,
Forever we will cherish
The kingdom we inherit.

Who disbelieves this boundless grace
Continues in transgression,
Is banished from the Father's face,
Has death for his possession.
His piety and active deed
Do him no good whatever;
His Adam-sin has sowed the seed
That ruins him forever
Without a hope of rescue.

The eye of man is but aware
Of plain clear water flowing,
But Spirit-given faith will dare
To see the crimson growing
From nail-marked hands to be the tide
That fills this stream with healing.
For sin and ills are turned aside
By God's sure Word revealing
That blood and water save us.

*Copyright © 1980 Concordia Publishing House*

# Christ with Death the Battle Fought
[*Jesus Christus, unser Heiland*]

Christ with death the battle fought
Gave His life, freedom bought,
And now is risen
From battlefield and prison.
   Kyrieleis!

Into no-man's-land He went,
Sinless blood for us spent.
God's wrath He carried,
Our guilt and death He buried.
   Kyrieleis!

All foes locked in narrow room,
Forth He stepped from the tomb.
That triumph moment
God sealed our full atonement.
   Kyrieleis!

*Copyright © F. Samuel Janzow*

## Come, Holy Ghost, God Our Friend
[*Komm, Heiliger Geist, Herre Gott*]

Come, Holy Ghost, God our Friend.
The fullness of Your graces send
To fill each faithful mind and heart;
Your radiant love to them impart.
Lord, welded by Your fire and light,
Men's souls in living faith unite
And learn to speak a common tongue.
For this, O Lord, Your highest praise be sung.
Alleluia! Alleluia!

O Light divine, Dawn of day,
Your Word of life shine on our way,
Reveal the true God, teach the art
To call Him Father from the heart.
All alien words keep from the throne,
That, ruled by Jesus Christ alone,
We live in faith, walk in the light,
And trust our gracious Lord with all our might.
Alleluia! Alleluia!

O Sacred Love, holy Fire,
With trust and joy our hearts inspire,
That loyal servants we remain,
Despite all tension, trial, and pain.
The Gospel's pow'r in us ignite,
Give courage for our faith's good fight
To take each challenge by God's grace
Till we, triumphant, stand before Your face.
Alleluia! Alleluia!

*Copyright © 1978 Concordia Publishing House*

# *Dear Christians, One and All, Rejoice*

[*Nun freut euch, liebe Christen g'mein*]

Dear Christians, one and all, rejoice
And set your spirits winging.
Let ev'ry faithful heart and voice
Unite in joyous singing.
And praise the wonders God has done,
How His love saved us through his Son
At cost too great to measure.

Once Satan held me in his pow'r,
Death was my prison-keeper,
Sin's brand on me since my birth hour
Each day burned ever deeper.
My struggling made me sink the more
My life was hollow at the core,
Sin's grip I could not loosen.

My mortal best in work or word
Was hopelessly corroded.
I thought God's judgment was absurd,
His pure command outmoded.
Yet fear drove me into despair,
I heard death's strident trumpet blare,
Hell's iron door swung open.

God from eternity had seen
My mis'rable condition.
By grace He willed to intervene
And send a rescue mission.
He was a Father deeply moved;
The depth of His concern He proved,
No cost He spared to help me.

He said to His beloved Son:
"It's time to have compassion.
My crowning Joy, You are the one
To bring man to salvation.
Go now and help man in his need;
For him slay death and all its seed,
Let him share Your life freely.

The Son His Father's will obeyed
And came to be my Brother,
To earth descended to be made
Man born of virgin mother.
He long concealed His mighty pow'r;
In servant's form He shaped the hour
For leading Satan captive.

I heard Christ say, "Hold on to me,
I'll lift you out of trouble;
Your Stand-in I myself will be,
I'll break your foes like stubble.
I'll ransom you and make you Mine,
At My high table you will dine,
The foe will never part us.

"The foe will wound Me, let My blood,
But when from life I'm parted,
Then from My death your life will bud.
Believe it, be strong-hearted.
My guiltless dying for your sin
From death your rescue will have been.
And you will live forever.

"Then to My Father I'll ascend
To claim you, who cost Me the most;
I'll be Your Master and your Friend.
I'll send my gift, the Holy Ghost;
Your strength and comfort He will be
And teach you how to follow Me
And show you truth and wisdom.

"Tell what I did and what I said,
Live by the Gospel story.
My Father's kingdom then will spread
To His great praise and glory.
Shun those who legal works impose
And spoil the work for which I rose;
This is My final counsel."

*Copyright © 1978 Concordia Publishing House*

## *From Darkest Canyon Depths of Woe*
[*Aus tiefer Not schrei' ich zu dir*]

From darkest canyon depths of woe,
O Lord, my voice is trying
To reach Your ear; O God, bend low
To hear my cries and sighing.
If You keep record of our sin
And hold against us what we've been,
Who then can stand before You?

Your grace and love alone avail
To blot sin out with pardon.
In Your gaze our best efforts pale,
Develop pride, and harden.
Before Your throne no man can boast
That he escaped sin's deadly coast.
Our haven is Your mercy.

In God I anchor all my trust,
Discarding my own merit.
His love holds firm, I therefore must
His fullest grace inherit.
He tells me, and my heart has heard,
The steadfast promise of His Word
That He's my help and haven.

Though help delays until the night
Or waits till morning waken,
My heart shall never doubt His might,
Nor think itself forsaken.
All you who are God's own indeed,
Born of the Spirit's Gospel seed,
Await His promised rescue.

Though sins arise like dunes of sand,
God's mercy-tides submerge them.
Like oceans pouring from His hand,
Strong flows the grace to purge them.
Our Shepherd will His Israel lead
To uplands out of ev'ry need
And ransom us from sinning.

*Copyright © 1978 Concordia Publishing House*

## *From Heaven Came the Angels Bright*
[*Vom Himmel kam der Engel Schar*]

From heaven came the angels bright
To shepherds watching through the night.
A newborn royal Child, they said,
Lies yonder in a manger bed.

To Bethlehem, King David's town,
As Micah saw, comes great renown;
Your Lord Christ is incarnate there
To save you all from sin and care.

Rejoice, therefore, that through His Son
Your God with you is now at one.
He took on human flesh and bone,
And you, His brothers, are God's own.

God came to share Himself with you,
Your sin and death He overthrew.
The foe his fiery darts may send;
Your shield is God the Son, your Friend.

He never will abandon you.
Trust Him, He's faithful, strong, and true.
Though all men scorn you, tempt, and mock,
God loves you; build upon that Rock.

Then in the end you will prevail;
God's friends and brothers cannot fail.
In praise to God then raise your voice,
Prepare forever to rejoice.

*Copyright © 1978 Concordia Publishing House*

# *From Heav'n I Come Here Singing Down*
[*Vom Himmel hoch da komm ich her*]

"From heav'n I come here singing down
God's joy on ev'ry field and town;
My news is of a wondrous thing,
Glad tidings of great joy I bring.

"A child was born this day to you
By God's own choice from virgin true.
A lovely Child! Or rather say
Starlight in darkness! Sun by day!

"For this is Christ, our God and Lord,
Himself your Helper and the Word
To heal whatever hurts have been
With snow-pure cov'ring for your sin.

"The blessings which the Father planned
The Son holds in His infant hand
To give to you that you may share
In heav'n the good things waiting there.

"Now listen what the sign will be
To let you know that it is He:
Plain cloth enwraps, a crib enfolds
The Child who all the world upholds."

Let us be glad about this word
And go to see what we have heard.
God, lead us in where shepherds went,
Show us the Gift Your love has sent.

Look, look dear heart, look over there!
Who lies within that manger bare?
What prince is lovelier than He?
The holy Christ Child this must be.

O Jesus, welcome, royal Friend,
Who came our broken lives to mend.
You turned not from my need away.
How can my thanks such love repay?

O Lord, Creator of the sky,
How low you bend who are so high;
Dry, withered field grass lines your bed
Where lowing cattle lately fed.

Expand this world a thousandfold,
Deck it with jewels and with gold,
Too narrow still that crib would be,
Too poor for Lord of land and sea.

No silk or satin for your bed;
Your throne rough straw in cattle shed.
But rich the glory of the grace
That fills Your throne room in this place.

From this dim manger light shines clear
To help me read the truth taught here
That worldly riches, honor, might,
Accomplish nothing in Your sight.

Ah, dearest Jesus, holy Child,
Make Thee a bed, soft, undefiled,
Within my heart that it may be
A quiet chamber kept for Thee.

You came and freed my heart to sing
And leap for joy and praise my King:
I join the carolers who throng
To offer You that cradlesong.

To God in heaven glory be,
Who gave His own dear Son for me.
The angels celebrate His birth,
A new year dawns for this old earth.

*Copyright © 1978 Concordia Publishing House*

# God Blesses Those Who Walk His Way
[*Wohl dem der in Gottes Furcht*]

God blesses those who walk His way
And, trusting Him, His will obey
And work for their own livelihood.
Live so, and you will find life good.

Your wife will then your home entwine,
In good things fruitful like a vine,
And then your children, too, will be
Live branches on a healthy tree.

To bless you richly is God's plan
If you are a God-fearing man
And banish all the mighty ways
Which Un-men follow all their days.

From Zion's hill your God will bless
All that you do and give success.
Your city's peace will come again
When God is sought by faithful men.

A life in God is true success:
He comes with love, He stays to bless.
Your children's children then will be
True sons of peace and unity.

To God the Father be our praise,
And to His Son our thanks we raise,
And to the Spirit, three in one,
Who has His life in us begun.

*Copyright © 1979 Concordia Publishing House*

## *God, Holy Ghost, Creator, Come*
[*Komm, Gott Schöpfer Heiliger Geist*]

God, Holy Ghost, Creator, come,
Upon Your people's hearts descend,
Fill them with grace, and make Your home
In lives that You create and mend.

We name You Comfort ever true,
The welcome Gift from God above,
The healing Power ever new,
The Well of life and light and love.

Be to our minds a kindling flame,
And set our hearts with love aglow;
Uphold our weak and moral frame
Within the grace by which we grow.

Ringed with divine gifts sevenfold,
O Finger of God's own right hand,
By You is traced the Word when told
By tongues of fire in ev'ry land.

Drive far from us the cunning Foe,
And heal our wounds with grace and peace;
Map out the way we are to go,
And let our hurtful courses cease.

Show us our heav'nly Father's face
And Jesus Christ, His only Son;
Show us Yourself in all Your grace
That we to fullest faith be won.

We praise the Father and the Son
Who died and rose to be our Stay,
And God the Spirit, with them one,
Who leads us to eternal day.

*Copyright © 1978 Concordia Publishing House*

# God the Father, Be Our Shield
[*Gott der Vater wohn uns bei*]

God the Father, be our Shield
That nothing evil harm us.
Pardon sin that we be healed,
In death with strong faith arm us.
Save us from the devil's snare,
Keep firm our faith and holy,
Built on Your mercy solely
With steadfast heart and lowly.
Your strong armor let us wear,
With fellow Christians daring
To strike at Satan's snaring,
God's weapons manly bearing.
Amen, so then shall we dare
Triumphantly. Alleluia!

Christ the Savior, be our Shield
That nothing evil harm us;
Pardon sin that we be healed,
In death with strong faith arm us.
Save us from the devil's snare,
Keep firm our faith and holy,
Built on Your mercy solely
With steadfast heart and lowly.
Your strong armor let us wear,
With fellow Christians daring
To strike at Satan's snaring,
God's weapons manly bearing.
Amen, so then shall we dare
Triumphantly. Alleluia!

Holy Spirit, be our Shield
That nothing evil harm us;
Pardon sin that we be healed,
In death with strong faith arm us.
Save us from the devil's snare,
Keep firm our faith and holy,
Built on Your mercy solely
With steadfast heart and lowly.
Your strong armor let us wear,
With fellow Christians daring
To strike at Satan's snaring,
God's weapons manly bearing.
Amen, so then shall we dare
Triumphantly. Alleluia!

*Copyright © 1982 Concordia Publishing House*

# Here Is the Tenfold Sure Command
[*Dies sind die heiligen zehn Gebot*]

Here is the tenfold sure command
God gave to men of ev'ry land
Through faithful Moses standing high
On holy Mount Sinai.
Have mercy, Lord!

I, I alone, am God, your Lord;
All idols are to be abhorred.
Trust me, step boldly to my throne,
Sincerely love me alone.
Have mercy, Lord.

Do not my holy name disgrace,
Do not my Word of truth debase.
Praise only that as good and true
Which I myself say and do.
Have mercy, Lord!

And celebrate the worship day
That peace may fill your home, and pray
And put aside the word you do,
So that God may work in you.
Have mercy, Lord!

You are to honor and obey
Your parents, masters, ev'ry day,
Serve them each way that comes to hand;
You'll then live long in the land.
Have mercy, Lord!

Curb anger, do not harm or kill,
Hate not, repay not ill with ill.
Be patient and of gentle mind,
Convince your foe you are kind.
Have mercy, Lord!

Be faithful, keep the marriage vow;
The straying thought do not allow.
Keep all your conduct free from sin
By self-controlled discipline.
Have mercy, Lord!

You shall not steal or cheat away
What others worked for night and day,
But open up a gen'rous hand
To feed the poor in the land.
Have mercy, Lord!

A lying witness never be,
Nor foul your tongue with calumny.
The cause of innocence embrace,
The fallen shield from disgrace.
Have mercy, Lord!

The portion in your neighbor's lot,
His goods, home, wife, desire not.
Pray God he would your neighbor bless
As you yourself wish success.
Have mercy, Lord!

You have this law to see therein
That you have not been free from sin
But also that you clearly see
How pure toward God life should be.
Have mercy, Lord!

Lord Jesus, help us in our need;
Christ, you our go-between indeed.
Our works, how sinful, marred, unjust!
Christ, you our one hope and trust.
Have mercy, Lord!

*Copyright © 1980 Concordia Publishing House*

## *If God Were Not Beside Us Now*
[*Wär' Gott nicht mit uns diese Zeit*]

If God were not beside us now,
So Israel is saying,
If God were not beside us now,
Our state would be dismaying.
We are a weak and shrinking band
Looked down upon on ev'ry hand
By those bent to destroy us.

So set against us is their will
That, if God's help had tarried,
They would have ground us in their mill
And long since had us buried,
Like victims of a rolling tide
When sudden dark waves inland ride
To trample all beneath them.

Thanks be to God, who did not let
Their eager jawbones snatch us.
Like birds our souls escaped their net,
No snare of theirs can catch us.
Their traps are broken, we are free;
God stands beside us with the key
To His good earth and heaven.

*Copyright © 1979 Concordia Publishing House*

## *In Peace and Joy I Now Depart*
[*Mit Fried und Freud ich fahr dahin*]

In peace and joy I now depart
Since God so wills it.
Serene and confident my heart;
Stillness fills it.
For God promised death would be
No more than quiet slumber.

This is what you have done for me,
My faithful Savior.
In you, Lord, I was made to see
All God's favor.
I now know you as my life,
My help when I am dying.

It was God's love that sent you forth
As man's salvation,
Inviting to yourself the earth,
Ev'ry nation.
By your wholesome healing Word
Resounding round our planet.

You are the health and saving light
Of lands in darkness;
You feed and lighten those in night
With your kindness.
All God's people find in you
Their treasure, joy and glory.

*Copyright © 1979 Concordia Publishing House*

## *In the Very Midst of Life*

[*Mitten wir im Leben sind*]

In the very midst of life
Death has us surrounded.
Where shall we a helper find,
Hear his coming sounded?
For you, our Lord, we're waiting.
We sorrow that we left your path,
Doing what deserves your wrath.
Holy, most righteous God!
Holy, most mighty God!
Holy and most merciful Savior!
Forever our Lord!
Keep us from despairing
In the bitter pain of death.
Have mercy, O Lord!

In the midst of bitter death,
Sharp the hell-drawn harrow.
Who will break its teeth and save
Faith's most inner marrow?
Lord, you alone, our Savior.
Though you were grieved by our misdeed,
Pity drew you to our need.
Holy, most righteous God!
Holy, most mighty God!
Holy and most merciful Savior!
Forever our Lord!
Let despair not bind us
With its threats of deepest hell.
Have mercy, O Lord!

Through the midst of hells of fear
Our transgressions drive us.
Who will help us to escape,
Shield us, and revive us?
Lord, you alone, our Savior.
Your shed blood our salvation won;
Sin, death, hell are now undone.
Holy, most righteous God!
Holy, most mighty God!
Holy and most merciful Savior!
Forever our Lord!
Give us grace abounding;
Keep us, keep us in the faith.
Have mercy, Lord.

*Copyright © 1978 Concordia Publishing House*

# Isaiah, Mighty Seer, in Spirit Soared
[*Jesaia dem Propheten das geschah*]

Isaiah, mighty seer, in spirit soared,
And saw enthroned in majesty the Lord,
Around whose throne shone glory from His face,
Whose robe of light filled all the temple space.
Beside the throne two six-winged seraphim,
Who with their wings gave glory unto Him.
With two each veiled his face in holy awe,
And hid with two the feet that had no flaw,
And with the third wing-pair they rose on high
To span the heavens with this mighty cry:
"Holy is God, the Lord of Sabaoth!
Holy is God, the Lord of Sabaoth!
Holy is God, the Lord of Sabaoth!
His grace and might and glory fill the earth!"
Then shook the roof-beam and the lintel stone,
And smoke of incense swirled about the throne.

*Copyright © 1979 Concordia Publishing House*

## *Jesus Christ, Our Blessed Savior*
### [*Jesus Christus unser Heiland*]

Jesus Christ, our blessed Savior,
Turned away God's wrath forever;
By His bitter grief and woe
He saved us from the evil Foe.

He, to pledge His love undying,
Spreads this table, grace supplying,
Gives His body with the bread
And with the wine the blood He shed.

Banquet gifts God here is sharing;
Take them—after well preparing;
For if one does not believe,
Then death for life he shall receive.

Praise the Father, who from heaven
To his own this food has given,
Who, to mend what we have done,
Gave into death His only Son.

Firmly hold with faith unshaken
That this food is to be taken
By the sick who are distressed,
By hearts that long for peace and rest.

Agony and bitter labor
Were the cost of God's high favor;
Do not come if you suppose
You don't need Him who died and rose.

Christ says, "Come all ye that labor,
And receive my grace and favor;
They that feel no want nor ill
Need no physician's help nor skill."

If your heart this truth professes
And your mouth your sin confesses,
You will be your Savior's guest,
Be at His banquet truly blest.

Let this food your faith so nourish
That by love its fruit may flourish
And your neighbor learn from you
How much God's wondrous love can do.

*Copyright © 1980 Concordia Publishing House*

## Jesus Christ, Our Mighty King
[*Jesus Christus unser Heiland*]

Jesus Christ, our Mighty King,
Conquered death, broke its sting;
Now He is risen.
Our sin He left in prison.
Kyrieleison!

This Man without a stain
Took God's wrath, bore our pain,
Won restoration,
God's peace, a free salvation.
Kyrieleison!

Sin and death He holds at bay,
Opens up life's new day.
This very hour
Accept His saving power.
Kyrieleison!

*Copyright © 1978 Concordia Publishing House*

## Let Christ Be Glorified As Far
[*Christum wir sollen loben schon*]

Let Christ be glorified as far
As shines the sun or beams a star,
The Virgin Mary's first-born son
As far as roads or seaways run.

Our Maker, whose high praise we sing,
Took on a servant's form to bring
A sure redemption to all flesh
And render mankind sweet and fresh.

On this chaste mother God in love
Poured grace and kindness from above;
An infant life in her was sown
By Holy Spirit's pow'r alone.

Her body, like a soul, became
The temple of the Holy Name.
Her child was fathered by no man,
She bore God's Son by God's own plan.

The gentle mother then gave birth,
Her child the Lord of all the earth,
Foretold by Gabriel and adored
When John unborn leapt for his Lord.

In cattle shed Christ slept on hay,
In poverty saw light of day.
The Lord who shelters birds from harm
Lay nestled in His mother's arm.

The angels gathered in the sky
Their maker's grace to glorify.
Their joyful news the shepherds heard
And hastened to adore the Word.

Our adoration, too, ascends
To Mary's Child, our Lord, our Friend.
To God the Father we give praise,
And to the Spirit thanks we raise.

*Copyright © 1978 Concordia Publishing House*

# Lord God, Receive Our Praise and Adoration
[*Gott sei gelobet und gebenedeiet*]

Lord God, receive our praise and adoration
For this feast of our salvation.
Here we are nourished with Your body risen
From the death that was our prison.
Kyrieleison!
May Your body, Lord, born of Mary
That our sins and sorrows did carry,
And Your shedding of blood
Save us from the threat'ning flood.
Kyrieleison!

This holy body into death was given
To win life for us in heaven.
No greater blessing unto God could bind us
Than to taste this loving-kindness.
Kyrieleison!
Infinite the love we here ponder!
Your shed blood accomplished this wonder:
Bought from guilt our release
And restored us to God's peace.
Kyrieleison!

Grant by this meal, Lord, all Your grace and favor
That Your love guide our behavior
Toward truest brotherhood and loyal union
Growing strong through this communion.
Kyrieleison!
Let not Your good Spirit forsake us!
Grant that true and loving He make us;
Help Your Church, Lord, to see
Days of peace and unity.
Kyrieleison!

Copyright © 1979 Concordia Publishing House

# Lord God, We Sing Your Praise
# (The Te Deum)

[*Herr Gott, dich loben wir*]

Lord God, we sing Your praise;
Lord God, our thanks we raise.
Father eternal, true,
All creation worships You.
All angels and heav'nly throngs
Serve Your glory with their songs.
All cherubim and seraphim
With soaring voices sing the hymn:
Holy is God the Lord,
Holy is God the Lord,
Holy is God the Lord,
The Lord of Sabaoth.

Your glory, might, eternity
Fill heav'n and earth with majesty.
The twelve apostles raise their voice,
The holy prophets, too, rejoice.
Armies of noble martyrs throng
To glorify You, God, in song.
The holy Church throughout the world
Keeps Your high glory's praise unfurled.
To God the Father on the throne,

To You, only begotten Son,
To You, the Spirit, Comfort true,
We bring our praise and worship due.

O King of glory, blessed One,
You are the Father's only Son.
From a virgin You took Your birth
To save mankind in all the earth.
You trod on death for its defeat
That Your own at Your throne might meet.
You rule at the Father's right hand
With equal glory and command.
You will come back to earth again
To judge with majesty all man.

O Lord, then in the final flood
Save those You bought with Your own blood.
Bring us to heav'n to celebrate
With all those who Your help await.
Save us, Lord, with Your healing glance,
And bless Your own inheritance.
Watch over us and guard our day,
Raise us to glory, Lord, we pray.
To You our daily praise we bring,
To Your name constant honor sing.

Guard us, O Lord, we humbly pray,
And keep us safe from sin today.
O Lord, have mercy on us all,
Have mercy on us when we call.
Lord, turn us toward Your kindly face,
Our hope is only in Your grace.
Lord, on You we build all our trust;
Let us not perish in the dust. Amen.

Copyright © 1979 Concordia Publishing House

## Lord Jesus Christ, We Praise Your Name
[*Gelobet seist du, Jesu Christ*]

Lord Jesus Christ, we praise Your name;
A truly human Child, You came
Of Mary by the Holy Ghost,
Rejoicing all the angel host.
Kyrieleis!

The Virgin Mother lulls to sleep
The Lord who rules the cosmic deep;
She gazes on his infant face
While he upholds all time and space.
Kyrieleis!

The Prince, God's very Child, is here;
He tents among the sons of fear.
His banner leads us out of woe,
And to his royal hall we go.
Kyrieleis!

The Light Eternal shows the way;
He gives the world a better day.
His beams break through the curtained night
And makes us children of the light.
Kyrieleis!

His doing this for me and you
Has proved His love both great and true.
All Christians, then, be glad and say
Eternal thanks for Christmas Day.
Kyrieleis!

*Copyright © 1966 Concordia Publishing House*

## Lord, Keep Us Loyal to Your Word
[*Erhalt uns, Herr, bei deinem Wort*]

Lord, keep us loyal to Your Word;
Curb those intent by craft and sword
To thrust Christ Jesus, Your dear Son,
From off the throne His vict'ry won.

Lord Jesus Christ, now prove your might;
As Lord of lords, lead us aright.
Your Christendom shield and defend
Till endless triumph songs ascend.

O Comforter of truest worth,
Give one mind to Your own on earth.
Stand by us in the final night,
Lead us through death to life and light.

*Copyright © 1979 Concordia Publishing House*

## May God Take Us into His Grace
[*Es wolle Gott uns genädig sein*]

May God take us into his grace,
Pour blessing from his fountains,
And by the brightness of his face
Guide toward eternal mountains,
So that his saving acts we see
Wherein his love takes pleasure,
And Jesus' healing power be
Revealed in richest measure,
Converting every nation.

All people living on his globe,
Praise God with exultation!
The world puts on a festive robe
And sings its jubilation
That your rule, Lord, is strong and true
And curbs sin's evil hour.
Your Word stands guard and will renew
Your people's health and power
To live in your high upland.

Our praises grow from living roots
When we thank God by action,
Improve the field, grow righteous fruits
Drawn by the Word's attraction.
Oh, bless us, Father and the Son
And Spirit, ever holy.
May people ev'rywhere be won
To love and praise you truly.
Now say a heartfelt Amen.

Copyright © 1979 Concordia Publishing House

# My Bride, the Church, Is Dear to Me
[*Sie ist mir lieb, die werte Magd*]

My Bride, the Church, is dear to me
I never will forget her
Her lovely graces all can see.
I in my heart have set her,
My jewel fair
Has all my care.
When troubles come,
I have a home
Made lovely by her presence.
Her love and trust stand at my side,
Her service never lessens,
She makes my will her guide.

She wears a coronet of gold
In which twelve stars are beaming.
Pure like the sun her garments fold
About her, bright and gleaming.
The moon tides meet
Beneath her feet.
She is the Bride
At her Lord's side.
At last there comes the hour
When she brings forth her noble Son
In whom all see the power
Of God, the Holy One.

The dragon, full of ancient rage,
Would now the child devour,
But all the warfare he can wage
Ends in God's vict'ry hour.
The battle won,
God takes His Son
To heaven high
Beyond the sky.
The dragon fumes in fury.
Alone, what will the mother do?
Her God will guard her surely,
Her Father great and true.

*Copyright © 1982 Concordia Publishing House*

# *O God of Heaven, Look Down, Behold*
[*Ach Gott vom Himmel, sieh darein*]

O God of heav'n, look down, behold
Your people so forsaken,
How few remain in Your true fold.
Let Your compassion waken.
Men will not take Your Word as true,
And faith has almost vanished, too,
From all the human fam'ly.

Men echo subtleties they heard
Devised in hollow thinking;
Their hearts, not captive to the Word,
Resist true interlinking.
One points men here, another there,
And fanfare mouthings do not spare
Attempts to disunite us.

May God uproot all those who reach
For false and flimflam preaching,
Whose tongue declares in proudest speech:
"Who'll stop our latest teaching?
Now we will take things into hand,
Set up our own rule in the land;
We have no lord or master."

God therefore says, "I must arise,
The poor my help are needing;
I hear My people's painful sighs,
Complaints, and urgent pleading.
My saving Word shall enter in
And faith's good fight for them begin;
My Word will give them power."

As silver sev'n times furnace-tried
Is rendered purest metal,
So all who in God's Word abide
No trial can unsettle.
The cross imprints the mark of worth
And beams God's might through all the earth
To shine on ev'ry nation.

The Word, Your truth, O God, preserve
Against this generation.
May be from Your way never swerve
Through evil's infiltration.
For godlessness comes through the door
Where men Your holy Word ignore.
O Lord, defend Your people.

*Copyright © 1982 Concordia Publishing House*

# Oh, Grant Us Peace in Our Time, Lord
[*Verleih uns Frieden gnädiglich*]

Oh, grant us peace in our time, Lord,
Triumphant peace now lend us.
We have no other battle sword
Except the peace You send us.
You alone can save our causes.

To this our land and government
Give justice, peace, and order.
On life in Christ make us intent
To walk in our land's border
Ever upright, true, and godly. Amen.

*Copyright © 1982 Concordia Publishing House*

## *Our Father, Who from Heaven Above*

[*Vater unser im Himmelreich*]

Our Father, who from heav'n above
Has bidden us to dwell in love
And with our brothers gladly share
The burdens moving them to prayer,
Teach us no thoughtless word to say,
But from our inmost heart to pray.

Your name be hallowed. Help us, Lord,
In purity to keep Your Word,
That to the glory of Your name
We walk before You free from blame.
Let no false teaching us pervert;
All poor deluded souls convert.

Your kingdom come. Guard your domain
And Your eternal righteous reign.
The Holy Ghost enrich our day
With gifts attendant on our way.
Break Satan's pow'r, defeat his rage;
Preserve Your Church from age to age.

Your gracious will on earth be done
As it is done before Your throne,
That patiently we may obey
In good or bad times all You say.
Curb flesh and blood and ev'ry ill
That sets itself against Your will.

Give us this day our daily bread
And let us all be clothed and fed.
From warfare, rioting, and strife,
Disease, and famine, save our life,
That we in honest peace may live,
To care and greed no entrance give.

Forgive our sins and grace outpour
That they may trouble us no more;
We too will gladly those forgive
Who harm us by the way they live.
Help us in each community
To serve with love and unity.

Lead not into temptation, Lord,
Where our grim foe and all his horde
Would vex our souls on ev'ry hand.
Help us resist, help us to stand
Firm in the faith, armed with the might
The Spirit gives to sons of light.

Deliver us from evil days,
From every dark and trying maze.
Redeem us from eternal death,
Console us when we yield our breath.
Grant us at last a blessed end;
Receive our souls, O faithful Friend.

Amen, that is, it shall be so.
Make strong our faith that we may know
We must not doubt, but shall receive
All that we ask, if we believe.
On Your great promise we lay claim.
Our faith says amen, in Your name.

*Copyright © 1980 Concordia Publishing House*

# *Our Lord Lay Bound in Narrow Room*
[*Christ lag in Todesbanden*]

Our Lord lay bound in narrow room
To pay for our transgression,
But now is risen from the tomb
To make life our possession.
Let us then rejoice and bring
Our festive praises to the King
In soaring Alleluias. Alleluia!

Death's power none could overthrow,
All Adam's sons were helpless.
Our sin betrayed us to this foe,
For none of us is guiltless.
Death at once came through the gate,
Set up his rule to seal our fate.
And yet today we triumph. Alleluia!

When Jesus Christ, God's only Son,
For sinners substituted,
The vict'ry over sin He won
And thus Death's pow'r uprooted,
Struck him down and tolled the bell,
Declaring him an empty shell
Without sting, claims, or kingdom. Alleluia!

The strangest warfare there we see
Where Death with Life contended,
But Life secured the victory,
The reign of Death is ended.
Thus says God's inspired Scroll:
Christ's dying swallowed our death whole.
And drew its sting forever. Alleluia!

God gave His Paschal Lamb to be
Our Source of benediction,
Love shed His blood upon the tree
For us by crucifixion.
See, Christ's blood now marks the door.
Faith points to it, Death stalks no more,
The slayer cannot slay us. Alleluia!

So celebrate this festive day,
Rejoice in our Defender.
Sin's might He pierces with His ray,
Our Sun beams forth in splendor.
From the radiance of His grace
There shines a glory on each face
Turned toward His resurrection. Alleluia!

In joy we gather for the feast
And taste true Life together,
Instead of sin's old bitter yeast,
God's grace for ev'ry weather.
Christ will be our living Bread
And feed our souls that once were dead.
By faith Christ lives within us. Alleluia!

*Copyright © 1978 Concordia Publishing House*

## *The Unwise Tongue of Man May Say*
[*Es spricht der Unweisen Mund wohl*]

The unwise tongue of man may say,
"We give God honor royal,"
But by their actions men display
A heart that is disloyal,
To God's most holy will untrue.
Our God abhors the things they do
When they abandon virtue.

Then God Himself from heaven looks down
To make a full inspection
Of city, country, hamlet, town,
To see if man's affection
Is centered in His Word and will
And if some can be found who still
Hold to His words and do them.

He sees none choosing His right way,
He finds them always swerving;
To left and right they go astray,
False trends and habits serving.
Not one of them lives truly right,
And yet they think their actions might
Receive God's benediction.

How long will man be self-deceived
With man-made works and striving?
They have too long God's people grieved
With sin-directed living.
In God they do not place their trust,
Nor kneel repentant in the dust.
Each thinks himself his savior.

The heart of man finds no true rest
In self-directed living.
Faith sees God's love is manifest
And imitates such giving.
The world, however, scorns this way,
Rejects all that God's people say,
And spurns the Lord we trust in.

Who helps God's people in their need?
Who rescues them from prison?
God comes with might in word and deed;
We live since Christ is risen.
For God has saved us through His Son,
And for His people Christ has won
The help for which we praise Him.

*Copyright © 1979 Concordia Publishing House*

## To You We Pray, God the Holy Ghost
[*Nun bitten wir den heiligen Geist*]

To you we pray, God the Holy Ghost,
For the true faith, which we need the most,
And Your presence guarding our journey's ending,
When our road homeward will be bending.
Kyrieleis!

O precious Light, Bringer of the day,
Show us Jesus as the one true Way,
That we know the Truth and the Life that sought us
And again to our homeland brought us.
Kyrieleis!

O sacred Love, set our hearts aglow,
Send tongues of fire, words by which to grow,
That with hearts united we love each other
And remain at peace with our brother.
Kyrieleis!

O highest Comfort in deepest need,
Save from fear of shame and death, we plead.
When at last the Foe comes up to assail us,
Let the faith You gave then not fail us.
Kyrieleis!

*Copyright © 1979 Concordia Publishing House*

# *True God from All Eternity*

[*Der bist du drei in Einigkeit*]

True God from all eternity,
Three Persons in the Unity,
The sun departs at eve of day;
Oh, shed Your light upon our way.

We worship You when wakes the sun,
We kneel to you when day is done,
Our song ascends to praise Your name,
Now and forevermore the same.

To God the Father glory be,
And to the Son eternally,
And to our comfort, Holy Ghost,
From Your redeemed and faithful host.

*Copyright © 1982 Concordia Publishing House*

## We All Believe in One True God
[*Wir glauben all an einen Gott*]

We all believe in one true God,
Maker of the earth and heaven.
"Our Father," he would have us say;
Children's place to us has given.
He has pledged always to feed us,
Body, soul, to keep, to nourish.
Through all evil he will lead us,
Guards us well that we may flourish.
He cares for us by day and night
And governs all things by his might.

We all believe in Christ, his Son,
Whom as Lord we are addressing,
Of equal Godhead, throne, and might,
Source of ev'ry grace and blessing.
Born of Mary, virgin mother,
By the power of the Spirit,
Made true man, our human brother
Through whom sonship we inherit;
He, crucified for sinful men,
Through God's pow'r rose to life again.

We all confess the Holy Ghost,
Who grants comfort, grace, and power.
He, with the Father and the Son,
Robes us for the triumph hour,
Keeps the Church, his own creation,
In true unity of spirit;
Here forgiveness and salvation
Come to us through Jesus' merit.
The body ris'n, we then shall be
In life with God eternally. Amen.

*Copyright © 1980 Concordia Publishing House*

## We Praise, O Christ, Your Holy Name
[*Gelobet seist du, Jesus Christ*]

We praise, O Christ, your holy name.
Truly human child you came,
From virgin born; this word is true.
Your angels are rejoicing, too.
Alleluia!

Now in the manger one may see
God's Son from eternity,
The Gift from God's eternal throne
Here clothed in our poor flesh and bone.
Alleluia!

The virgin mother lulls to sleep
Him who rules the cosmic deep;
This Infant is the Lord of day,
Whom all the turning worlds obey.
Alleluia!

The Light Eternal, breaking through,
Made the world to gleam anew;
His beams have pierced the core of night,
He makes us children of the light.
Alleluia!

The Prince, God's very Son, came here,
Guest among the sons of fear.
His banner leads us out of woe,
And to his royal hall we go.
Alleluia!

Such grace toward us now fills with light
Length and breadth and depth and height!
O endless ages, raise your voice;
O Christendom, rejoice, rejoice!
Alleluia!

*Copyright © 1969 Concordia Publishing House*

## Why Would Foe Herod and His Horde
[*Was fürchtst du, Feind Herodes sehr*]

Why would foe Herod and his horde
So fear the birth of Christ our Lord?
Our Savior wants no earthly throne;
He reigns in faithful hearts alone.

A star led wise men from afar
To find the bright and morning star.
The three-fold noble gift they bring
Declares this Child God, Man, and King.

When baptized in the Jordan's wave
God's spotless Lamb assurance gave
That He had come to take our place,
Wash sin away, and bring us grace.

The living Word at Cana spoke
And water into wine awoke.
His Gospel word wakes hearts of men
To serve God's purposes again.

In jubilation thanks we bring
To virgin-born Lord Christ, our King.
The Father, Holy Ghost and He
Receive our praise eternally.

*Copyright © 1979 Concordia Publishing House*

# You Want to Live Your Life Aright
[*Mensch willst du leben seliglich*]

You want to live your life aright
Now and forever in God's sight?
Then these holy, these ten commands
Keep pure as God's will demands.
Kyrieleis!

I am your Lord, and I alone;
So worship at no other throne.
Trust me fully, and set apart
As my domain your own heart.
Kyrieleis!

In ev'ry need call on my name,
And in the world declare my fame.
Honor me with your worship true.
My grace will then work in you.
Kyrieleis!

Your parents honor and obey;
Serve me by serving them each day.
Be not angry and do not kill.
In marriage keep my pure will.
Kyrieleis!

The goods of others do not steal.
Speak truthful words, speak no one ill.
Covet nothing that's unallowed.
Give heed to God, not the crowd.
Kyrieleis!

*Copyright © 1980 Concordia Publishing House*

# TRANSLATIONS OF OTHER GERMAN HYMNS

# *All People, Now Make Ready*
[*Mit Ernst, ihr Menschenkinder—Valentin Thilo, Jr.*]

All people, now make ready
    Your hearts with true intent
That mankind's great Defender,
    Whom grace alone has sent
As Helper designate,
        In long since promised splendor
        Of life and light may enter
At every humble gate.

With all good will rebuilding
    The way for your great Guest,
Uproot what would distress Him,
    Upraise what lies depressed,
Make good the past neglect,
        Build up the sunken places,
        Of pride remove all traces,
The crooked redirect.

A humble heart before Him
    Stands high in His regard,
But hearts uplifted proudly
    Fear turns at length to shard.
A heart sincerely right
        That walks where God appointed
        The Spirit has anointed
For welcoming the Light.

Lord, in Thy high compassion
    Bend down with Advent grace,
Prepare me for the brightness
    Of mercy from Thy face.
Come from the thankless inn
        And make my heart Thy manger
      That I, no more a stranger,
My lasting praise begin.

*Copyright © 1966 Concordia Publishing House*

## Christ Is Arisen

[*Christ ist erstanden*—German hymn, ca. 1100]

Christ is arisen
From the grave's dark prison.
So let our song exulting rise:
Christ with comfort lights our eyes.
Alleluia!
All our hopes were ended
Had Jesus not ascended
From the grave triumphantly
Our never-ending life to be.
Alleluia! Alleluia!
Alleluia! Alleluia!
So let our song exulting rise:
Christ, our comfort, fills the skies.
Alleluia!

*Copyright © 1982 Concordia Publishing House*

# "Comfort, Comfort," Says the Voice

[*"Tröstet, tröstet," spricht der Herr*—Waldemar Rode]

"Comfort, comfort," says the voice,
"My people that they may rejoice."
The weight of sin, the judgment rod,
Removed by Christ, the Son of God.
Gladness, gladness let them hear,
With God's own peace the weary cheer:
"The prison's open, slaves are free,
Forgiven their iniquity."

Even, even out God's path,
Set straight what might invite his wrath.
The voice calls out, "Repent today,
The King of kings is on his way."

Witness, witness to the world
The glory of the Lord unfurled.
The hour now strikes, the dawnlight breaks,
God keeps the promises he makes.

Withered, withered human might,
Its bloom cut off by frost and blight.
All flesh, like grass, wilts to the core,
But God's Word lives forevermore.

Lift your voice, speak words of pow'r
That none may fear the awesome hour.
Now comes the Lord, your God is here,
His grace and might rule far and near.

*Copyright © 1982 Concordia Publishing House*

## Entrust Your Days and Burdens
[*Befiehl du deine Wege*—Paul Gerhardt]

Entrust your days and burdens
To God's most loving hand;
He cares for you while ruling
The sky, the sea, the land.
He that in clouds and tempest
Finds break-through for the sun
Will find right pathways for you
Till trav'ling days are done.

Rely on God your Savior
And find your life secure.
Make his work your foundation
That your work may endure.
No anxious thought, no worry,
No self-tormenting care
Can win your Father's favor;
His heart is moved by prayer.

Take heart, have hope, my spirit
And do not be afraid.
From any low depression,
Where agonies are made,
God's grace will lift you upward
On arms of saving might
Until the sun you hoped for
Delights your eager sight.

Leave all to God's direction;
His wisdom rules for you
In ways to rouse your wonder
At all his love can do.
When his plans are maturing,
Then wonder-working pow'rs
Will banish from your spirit
What gave you troubled hours.

How blest you heir of heaven
To hear the song resound
Of thanks and jubilation
When you with life are crowned.
In your right hand your maker
Will place the victor's palm,
And for God's great deliv'rance
You'll sing the vict'ry psalm.

Lord, till we see the ending
Of all this life's distress,
Faith's hand, love's sinews strengthen,
With joy our spirits bless.
As yours, we have committed
Ourselves into your care
On ways made sure to bring us
To heav'n to praise you there.

*Copyright © 1982 Concordia Publishing House*

## God Brought Me to This Time and Place
[*Bis hieher hat mich Gott gebracht*—Emilie Juliane]

God brought me to this time and place
Surrounded by his favor.
He guarded all my nights and days,
His kindness did not waver.
His peace as sentinel he gave
My spirit's health and joy to save,
To this day he has blessed me.

All honor, thanks, and praise to you,
O Father, God of heaven,
For mercies ev'ry morning new,
Which you have freely given.
Inscribe this on my memory:
My Lord has done great things for me;
To this day he has helped me.

Oh, help me ever, God of grace,
Through ev'ry time and season,
At ev'ry turn in ev'ry place—
Redemptive love the reason.
Through joy and pain and final breath
By Jesus' life and saving death
Help me as you have helped me.

*Copyright © 1982 Concordia Publishing House*

## Grant, Holy Ghost, that We Behold
[*Gott Heil'ger Geist, hilf uns mit Grund*—
Bartholomäus Ringwaldt]

Grant, Holy Ghost, that we behold
The grace of Christ, our Savior,
Whose wounds and agony untold
Make good for our behavior.
The last hour cannot bring us loss
When we are sheltered by the cross
That cancelled our transgressions.

Your living Word shine in our heart
And to a new life win us.
With seed of light implant the start
Of Christ-like deeds within us.
Help us uproot what is impure,
And while faith's fruits in us mature,
Prepare us for the harvest.

Then when our earthly course in run,
Death's bitter hour impending,
May your good work in us begun
Bring peace to our life's ending,
The joy of surely being brought,
By Christ, who our salvation bought,
Into our Father's mansion.

*Copyright © 1982 Concordia Publishing House*

## Grant, Lord Jesus, That My Healing
[*Jesu, deine tiefen Wunden*—Johann Heermann]

Grant, Lord Jesus, that my healing
In your hold wounds I find.
Cleanse my spirit, will, and feeling;
Heal my body, soul, and mind.
When some evil thought within
Tempts my wayward heart to sin,
Work in me for its eviction,
Weighted by your crucifixion.

If some lust in current fashion
Rises like a fi'ry flood,
Draw me to your cross and Passion,
Quench the fire, Lord, by your blood.
Lest I to the tempter yield,
Let me front him with the shield
Thorn-crowned, blood-marked tree displaying,
Sign the devils find dismaying.

Beckoned by the world's old question,
"Going my broad, easy road?"
Let me turn from its suggestion
To the agonizing load
Which for me you did endure.
Let me thus flee thoughts impure
Lest I toy with soiled emotions,
Losing joy in blest devotions.

Where the wound is and the hurting,
Pour in oil and cleansing wine.
Let your cross, its pow'r asserting,
Touch my life with grace divine.
Ev'ry bitter cup make sweet,
Bread of comfort let me eat.
For you won my soul's salvation
By your death for ev'ry nation.

Jesus, rock of strength, my tower,
In your death I put my trust.
When you died, death lost its power,
When you rose, it turned to dust.
Let your bitter agony,
Suffered for us, comfort me.
Dying, Lord, in its protection,
I have life and resurrection.

*Copyright © 1982 Concordia Publishing House*

## *Jesus, Shepherd, in Your Arms*

[*Guter Hirt, du hast gestillt*—Johann W. Meinhold]

Jesus, Shepherd, in your arms
You have held this child, once weeping,
Willed it should be free from harm
And the moaning end in sleeping,
Carried it then through the door
To where crying is no more.

There your peace ends ev'ry care;
No more wail of wind through stubble.
There bloom only meadows fair,
Never chilled by any trouble.
Your lamb, robed in radiant white,
Lives there, Lord, now crowned with light.

Shepherd us to that bright place,
Into fields where joy is ringing,
Where this lamb, in your embrace,
Has its sighs all turned to singing.
Bring us, like this child we love,
To that life in heaven above.

*Copyright © 1982 Concordia Publishing House*

# *Joseph*

[Traditional German carol]

Joseph! I'm here.
Has the promised little Child been born yet?
It's true. Where, then?
In Bethlehem, Judea
As records the prophet Micah.
Is it true? It is true.
Praise to God in the highest!

Joseph! I'm here.
May we see the promised little Child now?
Yes, do. Where, then?
Here in the cradle, as you see,
Wrapped in a warm, white cloth lies He.
Cradle Him. Here, look here.
Praise to God in the highest!

Joseph! I'm here.
Will you help me softly rock the Infant?
I will. Come then.
Lull, lullaby, O dearest Child;
Lull, lullaby, O Jesus mild.
Lulay, lu.
Praise to God in the highest!

*Copyright © 1971 Concordia Publishing House*

## Let All Together Praise Our God
[*Lobt Gott, ihr Christen alle gleich*—Nikolaus Herman]

Let all together praise our God
Before his glorious throne;
Today he opens heaven again
To give us his own Son.

The Father sends him from his throne
To be an infant small
And lie here poorly mangered now
In this cold, dismal stall.

Within an earthborn form he hides
His all-creating light;
To serve us all he humbly cloaks
The splendor of his might.

He undertakes a great exchange,
Puts on our human frame,
And in return gives us his realm,
His glory, and his name.

He is a servant, I a lord:
How great a mystery!
How strong the tender Christ Child's love!
No truer friend than he.

He is the Key, and he the Door
To blessed Paradise;
The angel bars the way no more,
To God our praises rise.

Your grace in lowliness revealed,
Lord Jesus, we adore,
And praise to God the Father yield
And Spirit evermore;
We praise you evermore. Amen.

*Copyright © 1969 Concordia Publishing House*

## Lift Up Your Heads, You Mighty Gates
[*Macht hoch die Tür, die Tor' macht weit*—George Weissel

Lift up your heads, you mighty gates!
Behold the King of glory waits.
The King of kings is drawing near,
The Savior of the world is here.
He brings salvation down to earth.
Greet him with shouts of holy mirth.
Our highest praise we bring,
Our God, Creator, King.

The righteous King is bringing peace;
He comes the pris'ners to release.
His royal crown, self-sacrifice,
Its jewel, mercy without price.
He brings our sorrows to an end.
Shout out with joy to God, our friend.
Our highest praise we bring,
Our God, Redeemer, King.

O happy town, O blessed land,
That keeps our gracious King's command,
And blest the heart when he comes in
His holy reign there to begin.
His entrance is the dawn of bliss;
He fills our lives and makes them his.
Our highest praise we bring,
God, Comforter, and King.

Unbar the gate, fling wide the door,
Your heart to God's design restore.
Adorn its walls with all things right,
With peace and love and joy and light.
Your King will then be glad to come
And live within you as his home.
Our highest praise we bring
To God, our Lord and King.

Christ Jesus, Lord and Savior, come,
I open wide my heart, your home.
Oh, enter with your radiant grace,
On my life's pattern shine your face,
And let your Holy Spirit guide
To gracious vistas rich and wide.
Our God, we praise your name,
Forevermore the same.

*Copyright © 1982 Concordia Publishing House*

## Lord Jesus Christ, Will You Not Stay

[*Ach bleib bei uns, Herr Jesu Christ*—Nikolaus Selnecker

Lord, Jesus Christ, will you not stay?
It is now toward the end of day.
Oh, let your Word, that saving light,
Shine forth undimmed into the night.

Rekindle for this end-time stress
Faith's ancient strength and steadfastness
That we keep pure till life is spent
Your holy Word and Sacrament.

To hope grown dim, to hearts turned cold
Speak tongues of fire and make us bold
To shine your Word of saving grace
Into each dark and loveless place.

May glorious truths that we have heard,
The bright lance of your mighty Word,
Spurn Satan that your church be strong,
Bold, unified in act and song.

Restrain, O Lord, the human pride
That seeks to thrust your truth aside
Or with some man-made thoughts or things
Would dim the words your Spirit sings.

The cause is yours, the glory too.
Then hear us, Lord, and keep us true,
Your Word alone our heart's defense.
The Church's glorious confidence.

*Copyright © 1982 Concordia Publishing House*

## *Manger and Word*

[*O Jesu Christ, dein Kripplein ist*—Paul Gerhardt]

Manger and Word
Cradle my Lord;
Here paradisal meadowlands will feed me.
In this glad place
I see God's face;
Here, clothed in human form, He comes to greet me.

Though wind and wave
Him homage gave,
He lent to bitter toil for slaves His Godhood.
The glorious Day
Took on our clay,
Like us was wrapped in weakness in His childhood.

Thy wholesome light
Illumes our night;
Thy strong and healing kindness is our tower.
Immanuel,
Thou art the well
Of joyous might that quells the devil's power.

O Christian, hear
This word of cheer
Look up, take heart, and put away depression:
Your Rescue came,
Gave you His name,
Joined you to God by His strong intercession.

Remember how
So wondrous now
His mercy raised you high above all sorrow.
The angel host
Will never boast
A joy to equal yours in heav'n's tomorrow.

Let worldlings keep
The crowns they reap.
But you, secure your Treasure, your Defender.
To him hold fast
Until at last
He shares with you His coronation splendor.

*Copyright © F. Samuel Janzow*

## Now Let Us Come Before Him
[*Nun lasst uns gehn und treten*—Paul Gerhardt]

Now let us come before him,
With song and prayer adore him
Who for our life has given
The strength we need from heaven.

The storms in battle clashing,
The hooves of thunder crashing,
True mothers guard the slumber
Of children without number.

So when events are fright'ning
And slash like lurid lightning,
God hides us in embraces
To shield his children's faces.

God helps all those forsaken
When to their plight they waken,
Our counselor, our treasure,
Our friend in pain or pleasure.

Lord, show your tender feeling;
For sickness give your healing;
To minds, when dark thoughts frighten,
Come with your joy, bring light in.

Above all else, Lord, send us
Your Spirit to attend us,
His peace in us abiding,
Our footsteps heav'nward guiding.

*Copyright © 1982 Concordia Publishing House*

# Now Sing We, Now Rejoice

[*In dulci jubilo*—Medieval Latin hymn]

Now sing we, now rejoice
With heart and soul and voice.
Life's most precious treasure
Here poor in manger lies;
He brings purer pleasure
Than sunlight from the skies.
Christ is born today!
Christ is born today!

God's Son, come from above,
Your grace and saving love
To my spirit bringing,
O pure and holy Child,
Fill my heart with singing
For grace so great and mild.
Draw me, Lord, to you!
Draw me, Lord, to you!

We sing God's love divine
For us in Jesus shine.
Guilt of sin had taught us
But death and misery;
Then our Ransom bought us
God's bright eternity.
Oh, that we were there!
Oh, that we were there!

Where is that place so fair?
Oh, nowhere else but there
Where the angel voices
With God's redeemed unite,
Awed that he rejoices
To share his joy and light.
Oh, that we were there!
Oh, that we were there!

Copyright © 1982 Concordia Publishing House

## O Darkest Woe

[*O Traurigkeit*—Freidrich von Spee and Johann Rist]

O darkest woe!
Tears, overflow!
What heavy grief we carry!
God the Father's only Son
In a grave lies buried.

Deep, deep the pain!
God's Son is slain,
The Lord, who came from heaven,
Who for us upon the cross
His dear life has given.

Our load of sin,
Our guilt within
Brought low him who is lying
In a stone-cold garden tomb,
Silent mid our sighing.

The Bridegroom dead!
The Lamb stained red,
His lifeblood freely flowing,
Wine poured out to cleanse our wound,
Health on us bestowing.

O Ground of faith,
Brought low in death!
Fair lips, your silence keeping.
Must not all throughout the world
Join in bitter weeping?

But how blest he
Eternally
Who here will rightly ponder
Why the Prince of Life has died,
Why God made this wonder!

O Jesus blest,
My help and rest,
My tears flow to entreat you:
Make me love you to the last
Till in heav'n I greet you.

*Copyright © 1982 Concordia Publishing House*

## *O People, Rise and Labor*
[*Mit Ernst, ihr Menschenkinder*—Valentin Thilo]

O people, rise and labor
To renovate the heart
That mankind's mighty Savior,
Whom God's love set apart
To free you all from sin,
May do the promised wonder
And with his life and splendor,
Victorious, enter in.

Prepare with earnest rigor
The way for your great guest.
Make straight his path with vigor,
Rebuild your lives with zest.
The sunken valleys fill,
Restore eroded places,
Where sinbursts leave their traces,
Cut down the prideful hill.

A heart that humbly serves him
Stands highest in his sight.
The haughty heart, the proud whim
Go down in anguished night.
But those who love God's Word
And go where he is pointing
Are fit by his anointing
To host their gracious Lord.

Dear Lord, in high compassion
Bend down with Advent grace.
My heart, I pray, refashion
With mercy from your face.
Come from the thankless inn
To make my heart your manger
That I, no more a stranger,
Eternal praise begin.

*Copyright © 1982 Concordia Publishing House*

## The Bridegroom Soon Will Call Us

[*Der Bräut'gam wird bald rufen*—Johann Walter]

The Bridegroom soon will call us,
"Come to the wedding feast."
May slumber not befall us
Nor watchfulness decrease.
But may our lamps be burning
With oil enough and more
That, with our Lord's returning,
We find an open door.

Then, oh, what jubilation
To see our Savior's face,
His glorious exaltation
Since winning us God's grace.
Then kings will come to meet us
And psalmists rich in song,
Apostles, prophets greet us,
A great and splendid throng.

Then Christ, his glory sharing,
Will give us crowns of gold
He won for us by wearing
Thorned agonies untold.
The Father with embraces
Will welcome us, each one,
Robed in the Spirit's graces
As princely as God's Son.

Like skies in joyous motion
Or music after tears,
New song will fill the ocean
Of heaven's ageless years
While angel hosts are raising
With saints from great to least
The anthem tides for praising
The Giver of this feast.

*Copyright © 1982 Concordia Publishing House*

## The Bridegroom's Voice Will Soon Be Heard
[*Der Bräut'gam wird bald rufen*—Johann Walter]

The Bridegroom's voice will soon be heard:
    "The wedding feast is spread."
Will those be there who have preferred
    To court dull sleep instead?
Lord, help us guard the sacred light,
    The oil supplied by grace,
Lamps glowing to await the bright
    Appearing of Your face.

What jubilation when our Lord,
    Whose blood and bitter pain
Unbarred high heaven's sin-locked door,
    In glory comes again!
His prophets, every patriarch,
    The psalmists with their song,
Apostles, all who wear His mark,
    Will march in splendid throng.

Then every faithful brow will learn
    The glory He has worn
Since He broke iron death to earn
    Our crowns on fields of thorn.
Our Father then will to His heart
    Receive us every one,
Clothe body, soul, and every part,
    As princely as His Son.

Then through the banquet hall will sound
    The music of the years,
The harmony that echoes round
    The singing of the spheres.
The cherubim and seraphim,
    All choirs west and east,
Will join our voices praising Him
    Who celebrates the feast.

*Copyright © F. Samuel Janzow*

# To Us a Little Child Is Born

[Anonymous]

To us a little Child is born—
The sun is not more glorious.
He is the Savior of the world,
Him angels hail victorious.

Be glad, be glad, O Virgin mild,
For joyous is the story:
You held and cradled in your arms
Christ Jesus, King of glory.

Now sleep, now sleep, my tiny Babe,
My Savior, Lord of heaven;
I now am yours, for You are mine,
Your life for me was given.

With joy let every heart o'erflow,
*Cantemus in choro,*
*In chordis et in organo,*
*Benedicamus Domino.*

*Copyright © 1971 Concordia Publishing House*

## Unite Your Voices, Praise Your God
[*Lobt Gott, ihr Christen alle gleich*—Nikolaus Herman]

Unite your voices; praise your God,
    Enthroned as Gracious One,
Who this day heaven's gate unbars
    To give us His own Son.

He issues from His Father's throne,
    Comes as an infant small,
And lies here poorly mangered now
    In this cold, dismal stall.

He wraps in frayed and lowly garb
    The splendor of His might;
A servant-image cloaks and dims
    The all-creating Light.

He undertakes a great exchange,
    Puts on our human frame,
And in return gives us His realm,
    His glory, and His name.

He is a servant, I a lord;
    Explain how this can be;
No love can match the Christ Child's love,
    There's none as kind as He.

He is the key and He the Door
    To blessed Paradise.
The angel bars the way no more,
    To God our thanks shall rise.

*Copyright © 1966 Concordia Publishing House*

## When I Suffer Pains and Losses
[*Warum sollt' ich mich denn grämen*—Paul Gerhardt]

When I suffer pains and losses,
Lord, be near,
Let me hear
Comfort under crosses.
Point me, Father, to the heaven
Which your Son
For me won
When his life was given.

Under burdens of cross-bearing,
Though the weight
May be great
Yet I'm not despairing.
You designed the cross you gave me;
Thus you know
All my woe
And how best to save me.

Christians, let us be undaunted.
Ev'ry day
Hurl away
That which once was haunted.
Is it true that death defeats us?
No! Rejoice,
For Christ's voice
Then in peace will greet us.

What at last does this world leave us
But a hand
Full of sand
Or some loss to grieve us?
See what rich and noble graces
Our Lord shares
With his heirs
In the heav'nly places.

Savior, Shepherd, my Defender,
I belong
To the throng
Blood-bought for that splendor.
Having you, I want no other
Light of heav'n
To be giv'n,
My dear God and Brother.

*Copyright © 1982 Concordia Publishing House*

# ORIGINAL HYMN TEXTS

# *Andrew, Hoping for the Kingdom*
(Andrew)

Andrew, hoping for the kingdom,
    Down along the Jordan trod,
Came and heard the Baptist pointing:
    "Christ, sin-bearing Lamb of God!"

Trust the lamb! Love Christ as Savior!
    Go then, do as Andrew did:
Tell another, bring your brother,
    Never let your light be hid.

Does your best seem much too meager
    Kingdom needs to satisfy?
Loaves that Andrew found fed thousands;
    Christ can make gifts multiply.

Andrew brought the Grecian strangers;
    They met Jesus face to face.
Share your Christ with every person,
    Any rank or age or race.

Be an Andrew! Tell another:
    "Jesus died for you and rose."
Cast the fish net, speak the Gospel.
    One by one the live catch grows.

Family, neighbor, stranger, bring them
    On evangelistic tide.
At the haven Christ will greet you
    With your catch he multiplied.

*Copyright © F. Samuel Janzow*

## *At Dawn When Came the Promised King*
(John the Baptist)

At dawn when came the promised King,
John's voice made all the desert ring:
"The Lord! Prepare the way! Repent!
Let your whole self for him be spent."

In him Elijah's spirit burned.
He scorned all sin, all sham he spurned.
With lashes of God's fiery wrath
He scourged the vipers from the path.

He cut through thickets gnarled with sin
To let the cleansing Gospel in;
Led penitents to that wide place
Where, baptized, they could grow in grace.

He preached the Lamb's high sacrifice,
The great amazing ransom price
That opens prison doors of night
And lets us walk the heights in light.

Dawn ever calls, when night is done,
"Rejoice! Here is the blessed sun."
Oh, heed the Baptist, greet our King,
Our saving Light, our winter's spring.

*Copyright © F. Samuel Janzow*

# "Be Practical," Our Philip Says
(Philip)

"Be practical," our Philip says,
    "For figures cannot lie."
But outward facts can blind our faith
    Till wonders pass us by.

When tested where to find the tools
    Which kingdom works require,
Shall we hold back because we lack
    The means that we desire?

Or does Christ wish us to begin
    With what we have at hand?
Should faith not simply trust in him
    For outcomes he has planned?

Our halting faith may limp and fail
    To leap from crest to crest,
But Jesus can work miracles
    And turn our least to best.

Like Philip we may strain to see
    The Father in his might;
Our earthbound minds need Jesus then
    To help faith master sight.

He says, "See me and so see God,
    His grace, his love immense."
Our Christ, his voice, his church, his work,
    These are the evidence.

*Copyright © F. Samuel Janzow*

## *Dear God, We Offer Thanks and Praise*
(Peter)

Dear God, we offer thanks and praise
    For Peter's Galilean life,
His boats and nets and working days,
    His friends, his loving wife.

A loyal man, yet in a wind
    Too like a wave that crests and falls.
Your grace his haven when he sinned,
    His anchorage in squalls.

Your Father's grace, Immanuel,
    Showed this impulsive man the rock
Where stands each faithful sentinel
    On duty with your flock.

There Peter stood when he confessed,
    "O Christ, God's Son; Redeemer, Lord."
On this great rock your church must rest
    To wield your Spirit's sword.

From that rock fallen, he was bold
    Denying you so cowardly!
Forgiven, charged to feed your fold,
    How firm his loyalty!

If we deny our Rock and fall,
    Reach, Holy Spirit, from above;
Lift us to hear Christ's mercies call
    Us back to faith and hope and love.

*Copyright © F. Samuel Janzow*

## *Dear Lord, Your Brother Known as James*
(James of Jerusalem)

Dear Lord, your brother known as James
Long spurned your Messianic claims.
His skepticism would not heal.
He scorned the Zebedees' warm zeal.

Your love, relentless, found the hour
To break with resurrection power
Through dismal unbelief's hard shell
That held James in a private hell.

Then, far above the outward name,
A loyal brother James became.
Jerusalem all saw him rise
To leadership, good, firm, and wise.

He led the Council which first said,
"Let Gentiles share our living bread."
Today help us his message heed:
"A living faith yields loving deed."

Lord, bless us, each one who affirms,
Like James, the Gospel's ageless terms:
"Live faith in Christ bears righteous fruits,
A holy life from grace-fed roots."

*Copyright © F. Samuel Janzow*

## *Enrolled with Christ's Eleven*
(Matthias)

Enrolled with Christ's Eleven
    The Traitor's place to fill,
Twelfth stone on which is founded
    God's house on Zion's hill.
His name but once recorded
    Upon the sacred page,
And yet for us Matthias
    Lives on from age to age.

Christ's life and power keep flowing
    Unseen through every cell
Of his one church, his body,
    But how no one can tell.
Our God alone keeps record
    What's said, prayed, planned, and done
By unknowns like Matthias
    Who live in Christ, his Son.

Each drop hid in the ocean
    Shares in its tidal might;
So Christ's resplendent glory
    Shines hid in sons of Light.
The world will keep no record
    Of all their faith and love,
But, oh, the joy when angels
    Display their deeds above.

*Copyright © F. Samuel Janzow*

# *From Shepherding of Stars*

From shepherding of stars that gaze
Toward heav'nly fields of light,
I come with tidings to amaze
You watchers of the night,
You watchers of the night.

Your shepherd King from starlit hall
Bends down to weary lands,
Lies mangered low in cattle stall.
Go touch his infant hands,
Go touch his infant hands.

This night your king brings from afar
The virgin's lullaby,
The Wise Men's faith, a guiding star,
And love from God Most High,
And love from God Most High.

He shepherds from the thistled place
The flocks by thickets torn;
His piercéd hands heal all your race
Sore wounded by the thorn,
Sore wounded by the thorn.

Embrace the Christ Child, and with songs
Bind up the hearts of men.
To shepherd-healer-king let throngs
Sing glorias again,
Sing glorias again.

*Copyright © 1963 Concordia Publishing House*

## *Gabriel, You Brought to Mary*

Gabriel, you brought to Mary
Word from God that by His grace
And the power of the Spirit
God the Son, to join our race,
Would be born child of the virgin.
Did her heart that truth embrace?
    She believed, and she rejoiced.

Messenger to troubled Joseph,
He with wonder heard you tell
That our God had chosen Mary
Mother of Immanuel.
Did he make his home their haven,
Trusting God in what befell?
    He believed, and he obeyed.

Angel from the brightest glory
Shining into darkest night,
When your dawnsong to the shepherds
Praised the coming of the Light—
"Christ is born to save from darkness!"—
Did they go to see the sight?
    They saw Daybreak, saw our Lord.

Holy Ghost, grant faith like Mary's
To believe we are God's choice
And belong to Him who called us;
Help us heed our Shepherd's voice
And obey like faithful Joseph,
And come flocking to rejoice
    With the shepherds of the Light.

*Copyright © 1976 Concordia Publishing House*

# God's Own Son Conceived in Mary
(Joseph)

"God's own Son conceived in Mary
    By the Spirit" was the word.
Joseph heard it from God's angel
    And believed what he had heard.

Oh, the greatness of the wonder,
    God is born as flesh and bone.
Our heart's faith is just as wondrous,
    Taking birth from God alone.

Where there's faith, obedience follows.
    Joseph acts on God's command:
Leads the family into safety
    With a strong and gentle hand.

Home from Egypt, in his workshop
    He earns them their daily bread,
Careful also that their spirits
    With the bread of life are fed.

He reflects God's plan for fathers,
    Shows to family heads their part.
Give us, Lord, such Josephs modeled
    After God our Father's heart.

*Copyright © F. Samuel Janzow*

## Great God, You Drew a Gleaming Earth
(Remembrance of Baptism)

Great God, you drew a gleaming earth
From primal waters at its birth
By pow'r of your creating word
To flash in sunlight like a bird.

Your Holy Spirit likewise drew
By word and water us to you.
His holy washing ends our night,
We rise newborn, we live in light.

We were dead clay until baptized
And by your gift of grace surprised.
Faith takes the gift, new life begins,
We walk away from former sins.

Our hearts once were an arid plain,
But deserts bloom when you send rain.
When pow'r of Baptism fills our days,
We learn your Spirit's holy ways.

Each day pours in the blessed flood
Of mercies won through Jesus' blood,
Yourself an ark through time and space
To keep us in baptismal grace.

Our life in you toward glory grows
Because salvation's water flows,
Like ocean currents round the earth,
And bears us toward our heav'nly birth.

*Copyright © F. Samuel Janzow*

# In Her Arms the Blessed Virgin
(The Presentation)

In her arms the blessed Virgin
    Bears good Joseph's foster child.
In the temple to his Father
    She presents the infant mild.
In this Christ, the world's Redeemer,
    Heav'n and earth are reconciled.

God made his own Son our brother.
    In this little child, God sent
Our Creator for our ransom
    That we rebels might repent,
Cradle in our hearts this infant,
    Trust God's love, and be content.

May our Simeon faith hold Jesus,
    Heaven's peace pledge, our delight,
Promised dawn of consolation
    In our watching through the night,
Faithful Israel's great glory,
King of nations, Lord of might.

Throngs rise up in faith to greet him,
    Others spurn him to his face.
Strong be our faith's hold to cherish
    This our Ransom, source of grace,
In the deep heart's core enfolding
    Him who won us God's embrace.

*Copyright © F. Samuel Janzow*

# Jesus Called, "James, Follow Me Now"
(James)

Jesus called, "James, follow me now;
    Leave the Sea of Galilee.
Cast the net God's grace has woven;
    Fish nets leave to Zebedee."—
Great the privilege Jesus offers:
    Toil on tides of humankind,
Drawing souls from seas of darkness
    Into peace for heart and mind.

Chosen for Christ's inner circle,
    Something special did James see?
Yes, Christ's splendor on the mountain;
    Then his garden agony.—
Everywhere faith sees Christ present,
    On dust road or mountain height.
Like his glory when transfigured,
    His "I'm with you" gives delight.

Shall we ask for other favors?
    Great rank at the King's right hand?
Special kingdom gifts or status
    When we reach the promised land?—
No, the honor in the kingdom
    Is self-giving loyalty.
Help me, Savior, serve your servants
    As he served and honored me.

Low you bent down from your glory,
    Washed me from my guilt of sin,
Promised me the Father's goodness
    In what will be or has been.
Like James' cup, will mine seem bitter?
    Will I lose this life and fame?
Then my joy be in my losses
    For the glory of your name.

*Copyright © F. Samuel Janzow*

## *Look Toward the Mountains*

Look toward the mountains of the Lord,
Rampart against the devil's horde;
Ascend the heights where God's adored.
Alleluia, alleluia, alleluia!

But our best banners tattered lie—
Dare we approach God's Sinai?
There thund'rous, love's ten standards fly.
Alleluia, alleluia, alleluia!

Holy the lightnings round them flare.
But higher, look, what glory there;
What Gospel trumpets fill the air!
Alleluia, alleluia, alleluia!

Oh, soaring mount of saving grace,
Where sin can never hide God's face,
Where all who come have his embrace!
Alleluia, alleluia, alleluia!

Christ is the way to that blest height!
Our wayward steps he sets aright,
He takes us up into the light.
Alleluia, alleluia, alleluia!

Follow the cross where God the Lord,
His Son, who life and joy restored,
And their blest Spirit are adored.
Alleluia, alleluia, alleluia!

*Copyright © 1982 Concordia Publishing House*

## Lord, for Saint Bartholomew

(Nathaniel Bartholomew)

Lord, for Saint Bartholomew
Our thanksgivings rise to you,
For in him you let us meet
Openness without deceit.

Philip said, "We found the king,
Him of whom the prophets sing.
He from Nazareth came down
Wearing King Messiah's crown."

The reply was, "Nazareth!
Source of royalty? No breath
Of that town in prophecy."
Philip said, "Just come and see."

Come he did with open mind.
Thus may we come, seek and find,
Hearing Christ say when we meet,
"Here is one without deceit."

Jesus knew Bartholomew
As he knows both me and you,
Sees wherever we may be
Sitting under our fig tree.

When he speaks, the heart should leap
With the Spirit's upward sweep:
"You are God's Son, Israel's King,
As we chosen people sing."

Looking farther, may we see
Far beyond our own fig tree:
Heaven open, pouring grace
Everywhere on every race.

Copyright © F. Samuel Janzow

## *Lord, When You Came as Welcome Guest*

Lord, when You came as welcome guest
To Cana's wedding feast,
The bridal pair, divinely blest,
Found all their joy increased.

Now give your presence from above
That these, by vowing true,
May show their pledge is like the love
Between the Church and You.

Preserve the vow these two shall make,
This circle round their life,
This golden ring that none may break
Which makes them husband, wife.

Your daily mercies let them share,
All threats of harm destroy;
By this their vow divide their care
And double all their joy.

On all who thus before You kneel
Your joyous Spirit pour
That each may wake the other's zeal
To love you more and more.

O grant them here in peace to live,
In purity and love,
And after this life to receive
The crown of life above.

*Copyright © 1982 Concordia Publishing House*

## Lord, Your Young Follower, John Mark

(Mark)

Lord, your young follower, John Mark,
    Sustained a grievous loss
When losing his identity
    Through fleeing from his cross.

When from your will for us we flee
    And lose the cross from view,
Lord, let your mercy find us soon
    And draw us back to you.

Then quicken our slow pace to serve
    Your people when you call,
As Mark, restored, served Barnabas,
    Saint Peter and Saint Paul.

Your Spirit moved Mark's lively pen
    To trace your saving ways.
So may your living Gospel run
    Through pages of our days.

Imprint your image bold and clear
    On all our words and deeds
That aimless runners then may read
    In us the goal man needs.

*Copyright © F. Samuel Janzow*

# Mary Went Up To Hill Country

A Carol for the Visitation

Mary went up to hill country,
Elizabeth she came to see.
Her cousin's greeting which she heard
Came by the Spirit's inward word:
"You are the mother of my King."
Then sweetly did the Virgin sing:
My heart God's greatness voices,
My soul in Him rejoices.
He is my Savior, faithful, true;
His mercy will enfold you too.

Stay-at-homes never let us be,
But go we up through hill country
And there speak kindly, each to each,
The Spirit's greeting that can reach
The heart and open it to sing
The song that only faith can bring:
My heart God's greatness voices,
My soul in Him rejoices.
He is my Savior, faithful, true;
His mercy will enfold you too.

*Copyright © 1971 Concordia Publishing House*

## *Nunc Dimittis*

A deep-sea calm from wells of joy
Flows through my spirit.
No surface winds my soul annoy;
Thy peace fills it.
On my shoulder Thy hand rests
To gladden my leave-taking.

New dawn resplendent greets the eyes
At Christ's appearing.
With joy I from the dust arise,
Splendor wearing.
Lord, my Savior, gladsome Light,
Thou art the world's true Sunrise.

*Copyright © F. Samuel Janzow*

# O Christ, Our Consolation

(Barnabas)

O Christ, our consolation,
    Your name we laud and bless
For shining your compassion
    Forth through your Barnabas.
He knew how to be gentle
    With a converted Saul
And to your people's pillars
    Brought persecutor Paul.

Paul long in Tarsus waited
    For signals, to begin
His journeys and his labor
    The Gentile world to win.
When Barnabas then beckoned,
    "Come, you are needed now,"
The two long teamed together
    And pulled the selfsame plow.

His charm and wealth and status
    Good Barnabas applied
To serve Christ's great commission
    And swell the Gospel tide.
O Christ, inspire us likewise
    To open up new fields
That Gospel seed be planted
    For heaven's harvest-yields.

*Copyright © F. Samuel Janzow*

# O Gladsome Light of Grace
*(Phos hilaron)*

O gladsome light of grace
From God the Father's face,
World's morning star and splendor,
Blest glory of the day,
Night's pure celestial ray,
Our Christ, our joy, our Savior.

To Jesus Christ belong
Our voices filled with song.
Eternal source and river
Of mercy from on high,
Lord, you we glorify,
The whole world's true Life-giver.

*Copyright © 1975 Augsburg Publishing House*

# *O Jesus, Mighty Conqueror*
(Mary Magdalene)

O Jesus, mighty conqueror,
    The victor over hell,
Against dark fires protect our souls
    And watchful in us dwell.

Your might drove seven evil ones
    From Mary Magdalene.
Forgive, remove our hell-bent sin.
    Your presence keep us clean.

Our gratitude will then well up
    As from a crystal spring,
And like a lark in morning light
    Our hearts for joy will sing.

But when in grief our hope has fled
    And tears like Mary's flow,
Oh, show your presence, speak to us
    Till joys revive and grow.

We dare not touch your chosen course
    To bend it by our might.
Our glory be your winsome grace
    Surrounding us with light.

*Copyright © F. Samuel Janzow*

## *O Light of Light, Your Splendor Bright*
(The Transfiguration)

O Light of Light, your splendor bright
You showed upon the mountain height
To chosen men of Galilee.
Surround us too with radiancy.

What Moses and Elijah saw,
What filled your closest friends with awe,
What made their joy to overrun,
Reveal its hidden glowing sun.

Display a glory brighter far
Than planet earth's great golden star;
More bright than shines from heav'n above
God's holy tenfold law of love.

Your glory's crown was in your word
When with your prophets you conferred.
You there made Golgotha the key
And splendor of your ministry.

Your cross is heaven's glory gate,
A mercy infinitely great,
Self-giving love's most precious gem,
Divine compassion's diadem.

We chosen valley-born rejoice
At your dear heav'nly Father's voice:
"Oh, hear my glorious only Son;
Accept your ransom which he won."

*Copyright © F. Samuel Janzow*

## *Physician Luke Delights to Tell*
(Luke)

Physician Luke delights to tell
How you, his Master, makes us well.
His writing brilliantly defines
Your saving health, the light that shines
God's full compassion, care, and grace
On us, O Savior, from your face.

Such ills as doctors hope to treat,
Or such where science meets defeat,
The fears that crush, the hopes that wilt,
The failing heart, the fevered guilt,
All such you cover in your plan
Of healing for the whole of man.

Your Luke displays your Saviorhood
For rich and poor, for bad and good.
The Jew, the Gentile, woman, man,
The Pharisee, the publican,
If penitent, need have no fear,
For, Great Physician, you are near.

O Savior, Healer, mighty Lord,
In Luke the scalpel of your word
Probes deep to heal each special need.
There's life and health for all who heed
Luke's record with its saving facts
Of your and your Apostles' acts.

*Copyright © F. Samuel Janzow*

## *Praise God for John, Evangelist*
(John)

Praise God for John, Evangelist,
    Who bore the Spirit's sword,
Whose words reflect, like eagles' wings,
    The glory of the Lord.

Your brightness, O eternal Word,
    Apostle John unfurled,
The fullness of your grace and truth
    For us and all the world.

Your great I AM's Saint John records,
    Signs of your grace divine,
"I am the way, the truth, the life;
    The light; the living vine;

"Your soul's true bread; thirst-quenching stream.
    All these I am, and more:
The faithful shepherd of the flock,
    The sheepfold's only door."

O Word made flesh, your deeds and words
    Refresh our hearts like dew.
Our thanks we raise that all John writes
    Bears witness, Lord, to you.

We praise you that John's voice still lives
    Your glory to proclaim
Whereby your Spirit gives us life,
    The faith to bear your name.

*Copyright © F. Samuel Janzow*

## *Praise God the Holy Spirit*
(Stephen)

Praise God the Holy Spirit
    For granting from above
To followers of Jesus
    Faith filled with active love.
Thus Stephen by the Spirit
    Was filled with faith and zeal.
Elected by God's people,
    He served the common weal.

Praise God when faith like Stephen's
    Is willing to explore
How best to heal men's hurting
    And fractured peace restore.
When living word is wedded
    To thoughtful, active care,
God uses that blest union
    His grace and love to share.

Praise Christ, who grants the priv'lege
    Of standing firm with him
Against the darkness rising
    To make truth's sun grow dim.
When hailstone words come hurling
    To still our Gospel voice,
May we look up to Jesus
    Like Stephen and rejoice.

Saint Stephen saw Christ pleading
    For him at God's right hand.
From heaven he drew the courage
    In dauntless faith to stand.
So will our Lord sustain us
    When world would strike us down.
He raises us to glory
    And gives the promised crown.

*Copyright © F. Samuel Janzow*

## *The Magnificat*

My spirit magnifies the Lord,
My soul rejoices that God came
And noticed me of low estate
And lifted high my humble name.

His mercy toward the men of faith
Flows ever in abundant tide.
He saves them by his mighty arm,
He scatters all the men of pride.

His servant Israel he helped,
He kept his promises of grace,
Forgetting not a word he spoke
To Abraham and all his race.

## *The Very Skies Served You, O Lord*
(The Footwashing)

The very skies served you, O Lord;
All your commands the clouds obeyed;
Their rains refreshed the weary lands.
Yet your own hands once (like a maid
For sandalled guests come from the street)
Refreshed and washed your servants' feet.

In servanthood you stooped, sweat, bled,
To make God's temple holy, sweet.
In all its rooms no spot of sin,
No mud brought in from mart or street.
Our servant, Lord, you chose to be
To cleanse us from iniquity.

Your life and death dissolved our guilt;
We have your Father's dear embrace;
No trace of stain he finds in us
Since your baptizing brought us grace,
Washed us in mercy's boundless sea,
And clothed us in your purity.

In God's sight clean, forgiv'n by grace;
Yet sin's grime keeps collecting still.
Lord, daily gird yourself anew
To wash us and renew our will.
Oh, rid us of life's roadway dust.
Your daily cleansing hands we trust.

Refreshed each day by such a Lord,
We ever strive your will to please.
As you bend down in serving us
So we respond from bended knees:
Your servanthood we emulate
And wash the Lazarus at the gate.

*Copyright © F. Samuel Janzow*

## *Thy Planting*

Implant, O Lord,
Thy living Word
    In Adam's thistled dust
Of broken land.
Send Gospel rain,
Refresh the plain,
    Baptismal faith seed in
With thorn-pierced hand.

Thy Spirit's truth
Draw child and youth,
    Like grassland in the sun,
To strive toward Thee.
Their hope inspire
To tongues of fire,
    Each leaf-blade fed with wine
Of Calvary.

For glowing creed
And loyal deed
    Be Thou their Source and Sun,
Their living Vine.
Let Thy peace flow
That love may grow
    And harvest glory fill
Each branch of Thine.

Against the storm
That would unform
    Thy planting, make Thy cross
Their canopy,
Till heaven prolong
The vineyard song
    Of branches raised to share
Thy victory.

*Copyright © F. Samuel Janzow*

# *We Praise You, God the Father*

(Conversion of Saint Paul)

We praise you, God the Father,
    For Saul of Tarsus' birth,
An intellect of power,
    A mind of brilliant worth,
A conscience honed to sharpness
    By rigor of your law –
Yet only Jesus' glory
    His loveless heart could thaw.

O risen Christ, we thank you
    That you made him your Paul
When on his road you met him
    With love meant for us all.
Your foe there saw your glory,
    And more, your light of grace;
The merciless found mercy
    In you for all our race.

Employ, O Holy Spirit,
    Through Paul your word of pow'r
To turn us to our Savior
    For God's grace ev'ry hour.
Our God declares us righteous
    Belov'd in Christ the King.
This faith, alive and fruitful,
    Will make your angels sing.

*Copyright © F. Samuel Janzow*

# We Praise Your Call to Matthew
(Matthew)

We praise your call to Matthew,
    Who by your Spirit's choice
Left money-making madness
    To follow, Lord, your voice.
The new life you gave Matthew
    Became a banquet, spread
For publicans and sinners
    To taste the living bread.

We thank you, Lord, for using
    This man's bookkeeping pen
To write Messiah's story
    That saves the souls of men.
Oh, lest we think life's purpose
    Is wealth and worldly ways,
Illuminate its chapters
    With golden Gospel rays.

Life, fam'ly, friendships, business,
    Goods, money, talents, skill
Be wholly dedicated,
    Lord Jesus, to your will.
For you became our ransom,
    And we became your own,
The temples of your presence
    Where you are on the throne.

*Copyright © F. Samuel Janzow*

## When Christ Went Where He Would Be Slain
(Thomas)

When Christ went where he would be slain,
    His loyal Thomas said,
"Then let us go and die with him,"
    He knew Christ was the Head.

So let us walk with Christ our Lord
    Midst dangers loyally,
Prepared to give up life itself
    If that his will should be.

Our Lord will then show that he is
    The One who Godward leads,
The only Way, the Truth, the Life,
    God's answer to our needs.

Our senses tend to draw the blinds
    Against reality.
Oh, let faith penetrate to things
    That only faith can see.

True, Thomas, seeing Christ, believed
    What his own eyes had seen.
Most blest are those who trust the word;
    Their faith stays ever green.

Faith's firm foundation is God's word.
    God says what is, not seems,
And faith built on his bedrock facts
    Survives all doubts and dreams.

*Copyright © F. Samuel Janzow*

## *You Planted Us in Sun and Rain*

(Assignment to Ministry)

You planted us in sun and rain,
Your Gospel mercies fed our roots.
Transplant us to what field you will
To bear your Holy Spirit's fruits.

Let him fill our sin-furrowed lives
With flowing grace from Calv'ry hill
That we from root to furthest leaf
Grow up into God's holy will.

Let him whose nurture gives delight
Promote in us the Christ-like deed;
His winsome word make us to thrive
In faith that lives the saving creed.

Oh, let the Spirit's springtime ways
In us be brought to summer flow'r.
Let peace bloom fragrant where we go
To bring your wholeness, love, and pow'r.

We praise the Holy Trinity
For what has been and shall be done.
The Spirit's joyous fruit in us
Shall glorify God's blessed Son.

*Copyright © F. Samuel Janzow*

## *Your Jude and Zealot Simon*
(Simon and Jude)

Your Jude and Zealot Simon
    May represent the drive
Of those intent on helping
    Society survive.
But when some cause we stand for
    Conflicts with clashing views,
Then may our love not weaken
    Nor zeal our faith confuse.

Our Lord planned for His people
    Outward diversity
To stress his church's oneness,
    His body's harmony.
Let zeal for earthly causes
    Be caught up in one aim:
To be Christ's true disciples
    And glorify his name.

*Copyright © F. Samuel Janzow*

## *Your Mercy's Cup Has Quenched Our Thirst*
(Dedication to Service)

Your mercy's cup has quenched our thirst;
    You fed us, Lord, with living bread.
By joy refreshed, now let me work
    So that the hungry may be fed.

Estranged from God, we had no home;
    Your loving-kindness took us in.
I'll not turn strangers from my gate
    But shelter them as my own kin.

You stripped the soiled rags from our lives
    And robed us in your righteousness.
Let me then clothe the destitute
    And aid the helpless in distress.

When sick with sin we dying lay,
    Your pardon healed us, freed the soul.
I'll help my brother find the cure
    To make the mind and body whole.

Lord, oh, forgive where I failed You
    By failing those who are in need.
Grant grace, and make me fruitful grow
    A live tree sprung from Gospel seed.

At harvest may I hear You say,
    "A stranger, I came to your gate,
You quenched my thirst from your own cup,
    You stilled my hunger from your plate.

"You clothed me, tended me when ill;
    I was in prison, you brought cheer.
You did this, serving these my friends.
    Now see your kingdom! Enter here!"

*Copyright © F. Samuel Janzow*

# PSALM PARAPHRASES

# Psalm 1:
## How Blest, How Happy Is the Man

How blest, how happy is the man
Not bent by evil trends,
Nor caught up by what scorners do,
Nor bound to wicked friends.
He values what God's law commands
And makes it his delight.
He searches out the will of God
And follows what is right.

This man is rooted like a tree
Beside a wholesome stream;
His branches always yield good fruit,
His foliage stays green.
All that he does will prosper well.
The wicked are not so,
But, scattered by the wind like chaff,
Are driven to and fro.

Upon the final threshing floor
No godless men will stand,
Nor will they be among the grain
God gathers in his hand.
He guides his own upon right ways
And brings them safely home;
But all who take the evil way
Are going to their doom.

*Copyright © 1975 Augsburg Fortress*

## Psalm 23:
## The Lord's My Shepherd, See His Grace

The Lord's my Shepherd; see his grace
To me in kindness bending.
His care for me to Christ I trace
And know my cares are ending.

He guides to meadows on the height
Where living words are growing
And, brimming with the Spirit's light,
The healing brooks are flowing.

He leads on right paths, makes me strong
To follow to the mountains,
Breathe in his truth and sing his song
And drink from holy fountains.

When into shadows I descend,
My Shepherd walks beside me.
Against my fears his words defend
And through the valleys guide me.

Below, foes watch, foes of your flock,
The table you are hosting,
Set up for me upon the rock
Where friends your grace are toasting.

Eternal mercy opens up
The house of God the Giver.
His goodness overflows my cup.
I'm his houseguest forever.

*Copyright © 1975 Augsburg Fortress*

## Psalm 90:
## Our Holy Refuge on This Earth

Our holy refuge on this earth,
All generations' Lord,
Eternal God before the birth
Of mountains or the world,
No man refuses when you say,
"Return, O sons of men."
From age to age all him obey
Who turns us back to dust.

To you the thousand years long age
Is but as yesterday,
A night-watch dream, a cancelled page,
A sun-scorched blade of grass.
Your anger cuts into our days,
Your knife lays bare our sin.
We wilt away in your pure gaze
And wither toward our death.

Will none inquire why seven or eight
Times ten years fill life's span
With sweat or grief? O let us wait
Till God brings us to pray
At wisdom's gate: O Lord, relent,
Take pity, be our dawn,
Let your light, life and joy be sent
To fill our years with joy.

Awake us, Lord, to watch your hand
Do wonders in our lives.
Your offspring teach in ev'ry land
A morning song of joy.
Our life's dark places fill with light,
Show us your grace at work,
Remold our lives to bring delight
By deeds built to endure.

*Copyright © 1975 Augsburg Fortress*

# Psalm 93
## Clothed in Majesty and Light

Clothed in majesty and light,
His mighty power buckled on,
God fixed into his plan the earth
And built his throne into the dawn.

Oceans surge with clamors proud;
Loud clash world tumults mountain high.
When will the thunder chariots drown?
When word of God brings down the sky.

God's decree and law still fixed,
His will and promise firmly stand.
Their beauty shines where men obey;
Light beams from his house through the land.

*Copyright © 1975 Augsburg Fortress*

# *Psalm 95:1-7:*
# *Come, Join the Feast*

(The Venite)

Come, join the feast; come sing the praise
Of God our Lord and King.
Let joy around salvation's rock
Re-echo as we sing.
Your voices raise, like banners, high
As you approach the throne.
And with the trumpet's joyful noise
Give thanks for grace alone.

Great is our God above all thought,
Beyond all depth and height.
From his hands flow the oceans vast
Of atoms in their might.
Like winter-frosted clouds of breath
His word shapes galaxies
And patterns swirling stars like snow
O'er mountains, plains, and seas.

Like wheat before the wind, bend down,
Bow to the Lord above,
Whose Holy Spirit's bright wings spread
His glory and his love.
He sent his life into our clay,
Made us his very own;
He feeds and guards us as his flock,
Our Shepherd on the throne.

*Copyright © 1975 Augsburg Fortress*

## *Psalm 100:*
## *All Shades of Men from Dark to Light*

All shades of men from dark to light,
One fam'ly spread through ev'ry land,
O sing of God's creating might
Who fashioned you with loving hand.

He shaped his people in this mold,
We once were image of our God.
He now draws all who left his fold
Back to himself with shepherd's rod.

With singing let us enter, then,
The gate his mercy opens wide
And praise the love that calls all men
To stand forgiven at his side.

*Copyright © 1975 Augsburg Fortress*

## Psalm 103:
## He Lets Us See His Treasure

He lets us see his treasure
Of wise decrees and righteousness.
His love exceeds all measure,
He deeply pities our distress,
Nor treats us as we merit,
But lays his wrath aside,
Gives to the broken spirit
The grace that will abide,
And high as heaven above us,
As dawn from break of day,
So far, because he loves us,
He puts our sins away.

By his eternal grace alone
God holds his people in his love,
A love as steadfast as his throne
Toward those who seek the things above
And take him for their dwelling.
His rule is over all.
Angels in might excelling,
Bright hosts before him fall.
Praise him who reigns in glory,
All you who hear his Word.
My soul, repeat the story,
My soul, O bless the Lord.

*Copyright © 1975 Augsburg Fortress*

## Psalm 117:
## Praise Your Creator for the Day

Praise your Creator for the day,
Alleluia! Alleluia!
He breathed his life into your clay.
Alleluia! Alleluia!
Praise your Redeemer, God the Son,
Alleluia! Alleluia!
A princely place for you he won.
Alleluia! Alleluia!

Praise God the Spirit for his word,
Alleluia! Alleluia!
Proclaiming good news till you heard.
Alleluia! Alleluia!
The circle of God's love is strong.
Alleluia! Alleluia!
Praise him to whom you now belong.
Alleluia! Alleluia!

*Copyright © 1975 Augsburg Fortress*

# Psalm 121:
# Faithful Father, I Stand Pleading

Faithful Father, I stand pleading,
Helpless at your door of grace.
Often I ignored your leading,
From your kindness turned my face.
But life's lashing desert wind
Drove the truth home: I have sinned.
Now by your love drawn and driven
I return to be forgiven.

Faithful Savior, watchful keeper
Of God's people day and night,
As the dark'ning way grows steeper,
Lead and guard me with your light.
Sentinel against all hurt,
Let your voice keep me alert.
Shepherd me from sin-clogged sadness
To eternal upland gladness.

Faithful Spirit, stir these embers,
Pour your joy on me anew
Till my faith, aglow, remembers
How to rise and follow through
On the course it is to run
Where the Father's first-born Son
Set the pace and showed the manner
I must bear both cross and banner.

*Copyright © 1975 Augsburg Fortress*

# Notes on the Texts

## TRANSLATIONS OF LUTHER'S HYMNS

### A Mighty Fortress Is Our God (I)

This, the first of three Janzow translations of *Ein feste Burg*, appeared in *Church Music* (70.1) in 1970.

### A Mighty Fortress Is Our God (II)

This second translation of *Ein feste Burg* was first published in *Church Music* (75.1) in 1975 and was later reprinted in volume VI of *The Hymns of Martin Luther* (1982).

### A Mighty Fortress Is Our God (III)

Janzow's third translation of *Ein feste Burg* appeared in 1983 in the volume *Sing Glorias for All His Saints*.

### A New Song Now Shall Be Begun

This translation of *Ein neues Lied wir haben an,* a ballad celebrating the death of martyrs Heinrich Voes and Johann Esch in Brussels, was published in Volume VI of *The Hymns of Martin Luther* in 1982.

### All Glory Be to God Alone

The first publication of this translation of *All Ehr und Lob soll Gottes sein* occurred in *Motif* in the spring of 1975. It was reprinted in Volume III of *The Hymns of Martin Luther* in 1979.

### All the Nations' Savior, Come

This translation of *Nun komm, der Heiden Heiland,* completed by 1976, was published in Volume I of *The Hymns of Martin Luther* in 1978. It appears, in altered form, in *Lutheran Worship* as "Savior of the Nations, Come" (*LW* 13).

*LW* tune: NUN KOMM, DER HEIDEN HEILAND.

### Christ Jesus to the Jordan Came

This translation of *Christ, unser Herr, zum Jordan kam* was published in Volume V of *The Hymns of Martin Luther* in 1980. The text was completed by 1976.

### Christ with Death the Battle Fought

This early translation of *Jesus Christus, unser Heiland* appeared only in the Winter 1969-70 edition of *Motif.* Janzow's later translation of this text is entitled "Jesus Christ, our Mighty King."

### Come, Holy Ghost, God our Friend

Janzow's translation of *Komm, Heiliger Geist, Herre Gott,* written by 1976, was published in Volume II of *The Hymns of Martin Luther* in 1978.

### Dear Christians, One and All, Rejoice

This translation of *Nun freut euch, liebe Christen g'mein* appeared in Volume II of *The Hymns of Martin Luther* in 1978.

### From Darkest Canyon Depths of Woe

The first publication of this translation of *Aus tiefer Not schrei' ich zu dir* occurred in *Church Music* (73.1) in 1973. It was reprinted in Volume II of *The Hymns of Martin Luther* in 1978. In 1975, stanzas 1, 3, and 5 were reprinted as the metrical paraphrase verses of Psalm 130 (with alternating chant verses) in *Psalms for the Church Year* (Augsburg). The fifth stanza of the Augsburg version, however, included these textual variants:

Though sins arose like dunes of sand,
His mercy tides rise higher.
Grace flows like oceans from his hand,
Submerging wildest mire.
Our Shepherd will to uplands lead
His Israel out of ev'ry need
And ransom us from sinning.

### From Heaven Came the Angels Bright

This translation of *Von Himmel kam der Engel Schar,* completed by 1976, was published in Volume I of *The Hymns of Martin Luther* in 1978.

### From Heaven I Come Here Singing Down

Janzow first published a version of this translation of *Von Himmel hoch* in the magazine *This Day* in December, 1969. The opening line was "From heaven's star gate I sing down." Minor revisions were made to the text—including the first line—and the revised version was published in 1978 in Volume I of *The Hymns of Martin Luther.*

### God Blesses Those Who Walk His Way

This is a translation of Luther's paraphrase of Psalm 128, *Wohl dem, der in Gottes Furcht steht.* It appeared in Volume IV of *The Hymns of Martin Luther* in 1979. Stanzas 1, 2, and 5 had appeared earlier, as the metrical paraphrases of three verses of Psalm 128 in *Psalms for the Church Year* (1975). Janzow's unusual word "Un-men" (stanza three, line four) may be an allusion to C. S. Lewis's novel *Perelandra,* which Janzow taught. In this novel, the character of Weston, when taken over by the forces of evil, became known as the "Un-man."

### God Holy Ghost, Creator, Come

This is a translation of Luther's *Komm, Gott Schöpfer, Heiliger Geist,* which was Luther's translation of the ancient *Veni creator spiritus.* Janzow's English translation, composed by 1976, appeared in Volume II of *The Hymns of Martin Luther* in 1978.

## God the Father, Be Our Shield

This translation of *Gott der Vater wohn uns bei* was completed by 1976 and published in Volume VI of *The Hymns of Martin Luther* in 1982.

## Here Is the Tenfold Sure Command

This translation of Luther's hymn on the Ten Commandments, *Dies sind die heil'gen zehn Gebot,* is the text that appears as hymn 331 in *Lutheran Worship* (1982). An earlier version with minor differences appeared in Volume V of *The Hymns of Martin Luther* (1980), based on a 1976 text. The most noticeable difference appears in the title, which used the phrase "pure command" rather than "sure command." Verse ten originally began with the phrase "What you see on your neighbor's lot," rather than "The portion in your neighbor's lot."

*LW* tune: IN GOTTES NAMEN FAHREN WIR.

## If God Were Not Beside Us Now

Composed by 1976, this translation of *Wär Gott nicht mit uns diese Zeit* appeared in Volume IV of *The Hymns of Martin Luther* in 1979.

## In the Very Midst of Life

This text is the translation of *Mitten wir im Leben sind* that appears as hymn 265 in *Lutheran Worship* (1982). It includes minor changes to the 1976 translation that appeared in Volume 1 of *The Hymns of Martin Luther* in 1978. In addition to minor word changes, each of the expressions of "Have mercy, O Lord!" appeared as "Kyrieleison!" in the original version.

*LW* tune: MITTEN WIR IM LEBEN SIND.

## In Peace and Joy I Now Depart

Printed here is the translation of *Mit Fried und Freud ich fahr dahin* that appears as hymn 185 in *Lutheran Worship* (1982). An earlier version, with minor variations, appeared in Volume IV of *The Hymns of Martin Luther* in 1979. The original version began "With peace and joy," rather than "In peace and joy." The most salient change in the *LW* version is that stanzas 2-4 address Christ directly as "You," whereas the earlier version used "Christ" or "He" or "Him."

*LW* tune: MIT FRIED UND FREUD.

### Isaiah, Mighty Seer, in Spirit Soared

The translation of *Jesaia, dem Propheten, das geschah* printed here is the version that appeared in Volume III of *The Hymns of Martin Luther* in 1979. Janzow is also credited as translator of this hymn in *Lutheran Worship* (214), but the *LW* version was altered by editors.

*LW* tune: JESAIA, DEM PROPHETEN.

### Jesus Christ, Our Blessed Savior

This nine-stanza translation of *Jesus Christus, unser Heiland,* Luther's German version of John Hus's Latin hymn, appeared as hymns 236 and 237 in *Lutheran Worship* (1982). It was published earlier, with some variations, in a ten-stanza version in Volume V of *The Hymns of Martin Luther* (1980). Both versions, however, appear to be based on a 1969 translation that appeared in *Church Music* 69.2. In the earlier version, stanzas 6 and 7 were reversed, and the 1969 and 1980 versions included a stanza that read:

> Useless were for thee my Passion,
> If thy works thy weal could fashion.
> This feast is not spread for thee
> If thine own Savior thou wilt be.

*LW* tune: JESUS CHRISTUS, UNSER HEILAND

### Jesus Christ, Our Mighty King

Janzow published three identical versions of this translation of *Jesus Christus, unser Heiland.* The text appeared in *Motif* in the spring of 1975 and in *Church Music* in the same year (75.1). It was then reprinted in Volume II of *The Hymns of Martin Luther* (1978).

### Let Christ Be Glorified as Far

This translation of *Christum wir sollen loben schon* appeared in

Volume I of *The Hymns of Martin Luther* in 1978. It had been published earlier in a River Forest campus publication entitled *Celebrate the Joy of His Birth* (1972), a collection of Christmas hymns and carols to celebrate the 125th anniversary of the founding of the Lutheran Church–Missouri Synod.

## Lord God, Receive Our Praise and Adoration

This translation of *Gott sei gelobet und gebenedeiet* was published in this form in Volume III of *The Hymns of Martin Luther* in 1979. This version contains three stanzas. An earlier five-stanza version was published in *Church Music* (69.2) in 1969. It contained these two additional stanzas, as stanza 3 and 5, respectively:

> Praised be the mercy of our God and Savior!
> He did not spurn us forever,
> Nor punished us all our false and sinful living,
> But received us by forgiving.
>    Kyrieleison!
> Through Your holy sorrow and sighing,
> Crucifixion, agony, and dying,
> Be new life now supplied
> To the people at Your side.
>    Kyrieleison!

> Lord God, receive our praise and adoration
> For this feast of our salvation,
> Gift of Your kindness, rich and sacramental,
> Willed by action testamental.
>    Kyrieleison!
> At this banquet harvests are planted:
> Here Your people truly are granted
> Living Bread, life to give,
> Calv'ry's wine, that we may live.
>    Kyrieleison!

### Lord God, We Sing Your Praise

This translation of Luther's German version of the *Te Deum* (*Herr Gott, dich loben wir*), completed by 1976, appeared in Volume III of *The Hymns of Martin Luther* in 1979.

### Lord, Jesus Christ, We Praise Your Name

This version of *Gelobet seist du, Jesu Christ* was published in *Motif* in 1964 and reproduced in *Church Music* (66.1) in 1966. It provides an earlier—but distinctly different—version of the hymn that would become "We Praise, O Christ, Your Holy Name" in *Worship Supplement* (1969), *The Hymns of Martin Luther, Volume I* (1978), and *Lutheran Worship* 35 (1982).

### Lord, Keep Us Loyal to Your Word

This translation of *Erhalt uns, Herr, bei deinem Wort*, completed by 1976, was published in Volume III of *The Hymns of Martin Luther* in 1979.

### May God Take Us into His Grace

This version of *Es wolle uns Gott genädig sein* (a paraphrase of Psalm 67) was published in Volume IV of *The Hymns of Martin Luther* in 1979. It had appeared earlier in *Psalms for the Church Year* (Augsburg, 1975) as the metrical paraphrase of Psalm 67. It appeared as hymn 288 in *Lutheran Worship* (1982) in a version slightly altered by editors. The *LW* title is "May God Embrace Us with His Grace."

*LW* tune: ES WOLLE GOTT UNS GNÄDIG SEIN.

### My Bride, the Church, Is Dear to Me

Completed by 1976, this translation of Luther's *Sie ist mir lieb, die werte Magd*, was published in Volume VI of *The Hymns of Martin Luther* in 1982.

### O God of Heaven, Look Down, Behold

This translation of *Ach Gott von Himmel, sieh darein*, completed by 1976, was published in Volume VI of *The Hymns of Martin Luther* in 1982.

### Oh, Grant Us Peace in Our Time, Lord

This translation of *Verleih uns Frieden gnädiglich*, completed by 1976, appeared in Volume VI of *The Hymns of Martin Luther* in 1982.

### Our Father, Who from Heaven Above

Probably drafted by 1970, this translation of *Vater unser im Himmelreich* (Luther's hymn on the Lord's Prayer) appeared in Volume V of *The Hymns of Martin Luther* in 1980. A version of this hymn also appears in *Lutheran Worship* (1982) as Hymn 431, but the *LW* editors made some changes to the text published here.

*LW* tune: VATER UNSER.

### Our Lord Lay Bound in Narrow Room

This translation of *Christ lag in Todesbanden* was first published in *Church Music* (73.1) in 1973. It was reprinted in identical form in Volume II of *The Hymns of Martin Luther* in 1978.

### The Unwise Tongue of Man May Say

This translation of *Es spricht der Unweisen Mund wohl,* completed by 1976, was published in Volume IV of *The Hymns of Martin Luther* in 1979.

### To You We Pray, God the Holy Ghost

This translation of *Nun bitten wir den Heiligen Geist* was published in Volume III of *The Hymns of Martin Luther* in 1979.

### True God from All Eternity

Probably drafted by 1970, this translation of *Der bist du drei in Einigkeit* (Luther's last hymn) was published in Volume VI of *The Hymns of Martin Luther* in 1982.

## We All Believe in One True God

This translation of Luther's recasting of the Nicene Creed, *Wir glauben all an einen Gott,* appears as hymn 213 in *Lutheran Worship.* For *LW,* Janzow made minor changes to the translation he had published in Volume V of *The Hymns of Martin Luther* in 1980.

*LW* tune: WIR GLAUBEN ALL.

## We Praise, O Christ, Your Holy Name

This translation of *Gelobet seist du, Jesu Christ* appears as hymn 35 of *Lutheran Worship.* This is a revision, however, of an earlier version that was published as hymn 708 of *Worship Supplement* (1969). The *WS* version used "Kyrieleis!" to end each stanza, rather than "Alleluia!" It also included the following penultimate stanza, omitted in *LW:*

> To earth he came so poor to bring
> Great compassion as our King
> That rich in glory we might stand
> With angels in the heavenly land.
> Kyrieleis!

The translation from *Worship Supplement* also was used in Volume I of *The Hymns of Martin Luther* in 1978.

*LW* tune: GELOBET SEIST DU.

## Why Would Foe Herod and His Horde

Probably drafted by 1970, the translation of *Was fürchtst du, Feind Herodes, sehr* was first published in *Church Music* (75.1) in 1975. It was altered only slightly (the original title was "Why Does Foe Herod and His Horde") and republished in Volume IV of *The Hymns of Martin Luther* in 1982.

## You Want to Live Your Life Aright

This translation of *Mensch, willst du leben seliglich,* drafted by 1970 and completed by 1976, was published in Volume V of *The Hymns of Martin Luther* in 1980.

# OTHER GERMAN HYMN TRANSLATIONS

## All People, Now Make Ready

This is the first of two translations Janzow made of *Mit Ernst, ihr Menschenkinder* by Valentin Thilo, Jr. It appeared in *Church Music* (66.1) in 1966. A quite different version, entitled "O People, Rise and Labor," was included as hymn 25 in *Lutheran Worship* (1982).

## Christ Is Arisen

This translation of the anonymous German hymn *Christ ist erstanden* (ca. 1100) was published in *Lutheran Worship* (1982) as hymn 124.

*LW* tune: CHRIST IST ERSTANDEN.

## Comfort, Comfort Says the Voice

This translation of Waldemar Rode's *"Tröstet, tröstet" spricht der Herr* appeared as hymn 21 in *Lutheran Worship* (1982). It had been printed earlier in *Celebrate the Joy of His Birth*, a collection of Christmas music produced by Concordia—River Forest faculty in 1972 to celebrate the 125th anniversary of the founding of the Lutheran Church—Missouri Synod.

*LW* tune: TRÖSTET, TRÖSTET SPRICHT DER HERR.

## Entrust Your Days and Burdens

This translation of Paul Gerhardt's *Befiehl du deine Wege* was published in *Lutheran Worship* (1982) as hymn 427.

*LW* tune: HERZLICH TUT MICH VERLANGEN.

## God Brought Me to This Time and Place

Emilie Juliane's hymn *Bis hieher hat mich Gott gebracht* was translated by Janzow for *Lutheran Worship* (1982), where it appeared as hymn 456.

*LW* tune: ALLEIN IN DER HÖH.

## Grant, Holy Ghost, That We Behold
This translation of Bartholomäus Ringwaldt's *Gott Heil'ger Geist, hilf uns mit Grund* appeared in *Lutheran Worship* (1982) as hymn 336.
*LW* tune: ES IST GEWISSLICH.

## Grant, Lord Jesus, That My Healing
This translation of Johann Hermann's *Jesu, deine tiefen Wunden* appeared in *Lutheran Worship* (1982) as hymn 95.
*LW* tune: DER AM KREUZ.

## Jesus, Shepherd, in Your Arms
This translation/paraphrase of Johann W. Meinhold's *Guter Hirt, du hast gestillt* appeared in *Lutheran Worship* (1982) as hymn 269. The original German text was written by Meinhold to be sung for the burial of his own 15-month old son.
*LW* tune: MEINEN JESUM LASS ICH NICHT.

## Joseph
This translation of a traditional German carol was first published in *Make We Joy Now in This Fest,* published by CPH in 1971. It also appeared in 1972 in *Celebrate the Joy of His Birth,* a collection of Christmas music by Concordia—River Forest faculty that commemorated the 125th anniversary of the Lutheran Church—Missouri Synod.

## Let All Together Praise Our God
This is the only Janzow text to appear in four different Lutheran hymnals. This translation of Nikolaus Herman's *Lobt Gott, ihr Christen, alle gleich* was first published as hymn 712 in *Worship Supplement* (1969), and then as hymn 47 in *Lutheran Book of Worship* (1978)—one of only two Janzow texts in *LBW*. It was published in identical form in *Lutheran Worship* (1982) as hymn 44. It is also the most complete of Janzow's translations to appear in *Lutheran Service Book* (2006), which uses the entire translation (hymn 389) except

for stanza 2. This text borrows some material from Janzow's earlier translation of this hymn, entitled "Unite Your Voices, Praise Your God," published in *Church Music* (66.1) in 1966.

*LW* tune: LOBT GOTT, IHR CHRISTEN.

### Lift Up Your Heads, You Mighty Gates

This translation of George Weissel's advent hymn *Macht hoch die Tür* was published as hymn 23/24 in *Lutheran Worship* (1982).

*LW* tunes: MACHT HOCH DIE TÜR; MILWAUKEE.

### Lord Jesus Christ, Will You Not Stay

This translation of Nikolaus Selnecker's *Ach bleib bei uns, Herr Jesu Christ* appeared in *Lutheran Worship* (1982) as hymn 344.

*LW* tune: ACH BLEIB BEI UNS.

### Manger and Word

This translation of Paul Gerhardt's *O Jesu Christ, dein Kripplein ist* was published only in *Celebrate the Joy of His Birth* (1972), a collection of Christmas music by Concordia—River Forest faculty that commemorated the 125th anniversary of the Lutheran Church—Missouri Synod. It was a revision, however, of an earlier translation Janzow published in the Fall, 1964 issue of *Motif*.

Tune: O JESU CHRIST, DEIN KRIPPLEIN.

### Now Let Us Come Before Him

This translation of Paul Gerhardt's *Nun lasst uns gehn und treten* appeared as hymn 184 in *Lutheran Worship* (1982).

*LW* tune: NUN LASST UNS GOTT DEM HERREN.

### Now Sing We, Now Rejoice

Janzow's translation of the Medieval Latin carol *In dulci jubilo* appeared as hymn 47 in *Lutheran Worship* (1982).

*LW* tune: IN DULCI JUBILO.

## O Darkest Woe

Janzow contributed the first six of the seven stanzas of this translation, which was published in *Lutheran Worship* (1982) as hymn 122. The first stanza of the German text is by Friedrich von Spee, with the remaining stanzas by Johann Rist.

*LW* tune: O TRAURIGKEIT.

## O People, Rise and Labor

This text, the final of three translations Janzow made of Valentin Thilo's *Mit Ernst, ihr Menschenkinder,* was published as hymn 25 in *Lutheran Worship* (1982). The first version, "All People, Now Make Ready," appeared in *Church Music* (66.1) in 1966. The second incarnation, entitled "O People, Rise and Labor," was published in 1972 in *Celebrate the Joy of His Birth* (1972), a collection of Christmas music by Concordia—River Forest faculty that commemorated the 125th anniversary of the Lutheran Church—Missouri Synod. The final version in *LW* makes minor changes to the 1972 version. For example, the unusual phrase "where sinbursts leave their traces" (stanza 2 in *LW*) had earlier been "Where thrusting sin left traces."

*LW* tune: AUS MEINES HERZENS GRUNDE.

## The Bridegroom Soon Will Call Us

This translation of Johann Walter's *Der Bräut'gam wird bald rufen* appears as hymn 176 in *Lutheran Worship* (1982). The first stanza of this translation is reproduced in hymn 514 of *Lutheran Service Book* (2006). Janzow had published an earlier version—written in a slightly different meter—in volume 10 of *Motif* (Winter 1969-70) as "The Bridegroom's Voice Will Soon Be Heard" (see below).

*LW* tune: ACH GOTT VOM HIMMELREICHE.

## The Bridegroom's Voice Will Soon Be Heard

This translation of Johann Walter's *Der Bräut'gam wird bald rufen* was published in 1972 in *Celebrate the Joy of His Birth*, a collection of Christmas music by Concordia–River Forest faculty that commemorated the 125th anniversary of the Lutheran Church–Missouri Synod. It was based on an even earlier version that had appeared in volume 10 (Winter 1969-70) of *Motif*. This text was written to be sung to ACH GOTT VOM HIMMELREICHE, but only by adding extra syllables to eighth notes in lines 1, 3, 5, and 7, so that the meter is 8.6.8.6.D, rather than 7.6.7.6.D. A newer translation appeared as "The Bridegroom Soon Will Call Us" (hymn 176) in *Lutheran Worship* (1982).

### To Us a Little Child Is Born

Janzow published this translation of an anonymous German Christmas text in *Praises Ringing,* Book 8 of the Concordia Music Education Series *(CPH,* 1971).

### Unite Your Voices, Praise Our God

This is Janzow's first translation of Nikolaus Herman's *Lobt Gott, ihr Christen, alle gleich.* It was published in *Church Music* (66.1) in 1966. The revised version ("Let All Together Praise Our God") appeared as hymn 712 in *Worship Supplement* (1969), then as hymn 47 in *Lutheran Book of Worship* (1978), and finally as hymn 44 in *Lutheran Worship* (1982). Although the revised version seems superior on most counts, the third stanza may be more striking in this earlier version.

### When I Suffer Pains and Losses

This translation of Paul Gerhardt's text was published as hymn 423 in *Lutheran Worship* (1982).

*LW* tune: WARUM SOLLT ICH MICH DENN GRÄMEN.

# ORIGINAL HYMN TEXTS

*(With tune suggestions from David W. Rogner)*

### Andrew, Hoping for the Kingdom

This text, written for the feast of St. Andrew, was published in *Sing Glorias for All His Saints* (1983).

Suggested tunes: STUTTGART, RINGE RECHT, DOROTHY.

### At Dawn When Came the Promised King

Written to be sung on the festival of St. John the Baptist, this text appeared in *Sing Glorias for All His Saints* (1983).

Suggested tunes: TALLIS' CANON, WINCHESTER NEW, O HEILIGE DREIFALTIGKEIT.

### 'Be Practical,' our Philip Says

This text, written for the feast of St. Philip, was published in *Sing Glorias for All His Saints* (1983).

Suggested tunes: DUNDEE, WINCHESTER OLD, EVAN.

### Dear God, We Offer Thanks and Praise

Written for the feast of St. Peter, this text was published in *Sing Glorias for All His Saints* (1983).

Suggested tunes: ISLEWORTH, DUNSTAN.

### Dear Lord, Your Brother Known as James

Celebrating the ministry of St. James of Jerusalem (also known as James, the Brother of Jesus), this text was published in *Sing Glorias for All His Saints* (1983).

Suggested tunes: TALLIS' CANON, WINCHESTER NEW, O HEILIGE DREIFALTIGKEIT, WENN WIR IN HÖCHSTEN NÖTEN SEIN.

### Enrolled with Christ's Eleven

Written for the feast of St. Matthias, this text was published in *Sing Glorias for All His Saints* (1983).

Suggested tunes: AURELIA, KING'S LYNN, ELLACOMBE, MISSIONARY HYMN.

### From Shepherding of Stars

Written in 1962, a version of this text appeared in the Winter 1963 edition of *Motif* with the title "Evangel: Of Manger and Cross." The version printed here was first published in *Lutheran Education* in 1963, with a tune by Richard Hillert (SHEPHERDING). The text and tune were reprinted in *Worship Supplement* in 1969 (hymn 713), in *Lutheran Book of Worship* (1978) as hymn 63, and in *Lutheran Worship* (1982) as hymn 71. In 1996, Paul R. Otte published an analysis of this text (based on an interview with Janzow) in *Glad Tidings: The Story of Ten Carols,* published by Lutheran Hour Ministries. In 2014 CPH published a choral setting (with an original tune) by David von Kampen.

### Gabriel, You Brought to Mary

This text was first published in *Lutheran Education* in 1970, with a tune by Paul Bouman. It was reprinted in 1972 in *Celebrate the Joy of His Birth,* a collection of Christmas music by Concordia—River Forest faculty that commemorated the 125th anniversary of the Lutheran Church—Missouri Synod. In 1976 CPH included it in a small collection called *Bless the Manger-Child: A Collection of Twelve New Christmas Carols for Unison Voices*. CPH also published a choral setting of the hymn by Kevin Hildebrand in 2000.

### God's Own Son Conceived in Mary

Composed for the feast of St. Joseph, this text was published in *Sing Glorias for All His Saints* (1983).

Suggested tunes: STUTGART, RINGE RECHT, DOROTHY.

### Great God, You Drew a Gleaming Earth

This text was first published in *Sing Glorias for All His Saints* (1983) with the subtitle "Remembrance of Baptism." It was reprinted—with minor changes—in *Motif* in 1984, where it was subtitled "A Hymn on Baptism."

Suggested tunes: WINCHESTER NEW, PUER NOBIS, TALLIS' CANON.

### In Her Arms the Blessed Virgin

This text, written for the feast of the Presentation of our Lord, was published in *Sing Glorias for All His Saints* (1983).

Suggested tunes: SIER, HIER BIN ICH, REGENT SQUARE, WESTMINSTER ABBEY.

### Jesus Called, 'James, Follow Me Now'

Written for the feast of St. James the Elder, this text was published in *Sing Glorias for All His Saints* (1983).

Suggested tunes: HYFRYDOL, GALILEAN, REX GLORIAE, ABBOT'S LEIGH.

### Look Toward the Mountains

This text was published as hymn 310 in *Lutheran Worship* (1982), accompanied by Nikolaus Herman's tune ERSCHIENEN IS DER HERRLICH TAG. According to the *Lutheran Worship Hymnal Companion,* the hymn was "specifically intended as a processional or entrance hymn with banners and led by the cross on its way to the chancel."

### Lord, for Saint Bartholomew

Written for use on the feast of St. Bartholomew, this text was published in *Sing Glorias for All His Saints* in 1983.

Suggested tunes: BUCKLAND, ORIENTIS PARTIBUS, PATMOS.

## Lord, When You Came As Welcome Guest

This wedding hymn (a recasting of "Lord, Who at Cana's Wedding Feast", #620 in *The Lutheran Hymnal*) was originally written for the wedding of Janzow's son. It was published in *Lutheran Worship* (1982) as hymn 252. It was reprinted in *Lutheran Service Book* (2006) as hymn 859. It is the only original Janzow text in *LSB*. In 2004 CPH re-published the text in an SAB choral setting by Stephen Johnson.

*LW* tune: RESIGNATION; *LSB* TUNE: LAND OF REST.

## Lord, Your Young Follower, John Mark

This text was written for the feast of St. Mark, Evangelist. It was published in *Sing Glorias for All His Saints* in 1983.

Suggested tunes: DUNDEE, WINCHESTER OLD, LAND OF REST.

## Mary Went Up to Hill Country

This text for the Visitation was first published, with a tune by Carl Schalk, in *Make We Joy Now in This Fest*, published by CPH in 1971. It also appeared in 1972 in *Celebrate the Joy of His Birth*, a collection of Christmas music by Concordia—River Forest faculty that commemorated the 125th anniversary of the Lutheran Church—Missouri Synod. In both of these versions, the text was titled "Mary Went Up through Hill Country." The text was republished by CPH in 1994 as a choral anthem, in which the "through" in the title becomes "to," even though "through" remains in the second stanza. No other changes occur in the texts.

## *Nunc Dimittis*

This paraphrase of the Song of Simeon was published in 1972 in *Celebrate the Joy of His Birth*, a collection of Christmas music by Concordia—River Forest faculty that commemorated the 125th anniversary of the Lutheran Church—Missouri Synod.

### O Christ, Our Consolation

This text, composed for the feast of St. Barnabas, was published in *Sing Glorias for All His Saints* (1983).

Suggested tunes: AURELIA, ELLACOMBE, KING'S LYNN, MISSIONARY HYMN.

### O Gladsome Light of Grace

This metrical paraphrase of the *Phos hilaron* was published in *Psalms for the Church Year* (Augsburg, 1975) in a setting which alternated chanted lines of the *Nunc Dimittis* with Janzow's metrical paraphrase of the *Phos hilaron*. The opening lines appear to be based on Robert S. Bridges' translation of the Greek text (*LW* 486; *LSB* 888). It was paired with the tune NUNC DIMITTIS, in a setting by Claude Goudimel.

### O Jesus, Mighty Conqueror

Composed for the feast of St. Mary Magdalene, this text was published in *Sing Glorias for All His Saints* (1983).

Suggested tunes: DUNDEE, WINCHESTER OLD, ICH SINGE DIR.

### O Light of Light, Your Splendor Bright

A hymn for the festival of The Transfiguration, this text was published in *Sing Glorias for All His Saints* in 1983.

Suggested tunes: WINCHESTER NEW, O HEILIGE DREIFALTIGKEIT, WENN WIR IN HÖCHSTEN NÖTEN SEIN, WAREHAM.

### Physician Luke Delights to Tell

Written for the feast of St. Luke, Evangelist, this text was published in *Sing Glorias for All His Saints* in 1983.

Suggested tunes: RYBURN, ALL ERH UND LOB, MELITA.

## Praise God for John, Evangelist

This text, for the feast of St. John the Evangelist, was published in 1983 in *Sing Glorias for All His Saints*. It also was published in *The Hymnal 1982* (1985) of the Episcopal Church. There it appears as hymn 245, using the tune NOEL.

Other suggested tunes: ICH SINGE DIR, CAITHNESS, SHANTI.

## Praise God the Holy Spirit

Written for the feast of St. Stephen, this text was published in *Sing Glorias for All His Saints* (1983).

Suggested tunes: EWING, KING'S LYNN, MUNICH, MISSIONARY HYMN.

## The *Magnificat*

This version of the *Magnificat* was published in 1975 in *Psalms for the Church Year* (Augsburg)—along with *The Venite* and *The Nunc Dimittis*—at the conclusion of this collection of psalms. It was paired with a Michael Praetorius tune from *Musae Sionae*.

## The Very Skies Served You, O Lord

This Maundy Thursday text, focusing on Christ washing the disciples' feet, was published in *Sing Glorias for All His Saints* in 1983.

Suggested tunes: RYBURN, ALL ERH UND LOB.

## Thy Planting

This text appeared only in *Motif*, volume 10 (1969-70). The unusual meter (which could be described either as 4.4.6.4.4.4.6.4. or 8.10.8.10) does not seem to correspond to any existing hymn tune.

## We Praise You, God the Father

Written for the feast of the Conversion of St. Paul, this text appeared in *Sing Glorias for All His Saints* in 1983.

Suggested tunes: IST GOTT FÜR MICH, MISSIONARY HYMN, MUNICH, KUORTANE.

### We Praise Your Call to Matthew
Written for the feast of St. Matthew, this text was first published in *Sing Glorias for All His Saints* in 1983.
Suggested tunes: KUORTANE, MISSIONARY HYMN, MUNICH.

### When Christ Went Where He Would Be Slain
A hymn for the feast of St. Thomas, this text was published in *Sing Glorias for All His Saints* (1983).
Suggested tunes: CAITHNESS, DUNDEE, WINCHESTER OLD.

### You Planted Us in Sun and Rain
Subtitled "Assignment to Ministry" when it was published in *Sing Glorias for All His Saints* in 1983, this text was perhaps written to be used for "call day" services—or other occasions when people are commissioned into ministry. It might also be appropriate for graduations at Christian schools.
Suggested tunes: WAREHAM, LAKEWOOD, O HEILIGE DREIFALTIGKEIT, WINCHESTER NEW.

### Your Jude and Zealot Simon
Written for the feast of Saints Simon and Jude, this text was published in *Sing Glorias for All His Saints* in 1983.
Suggested tunes: MUNICH, KING'S LYNN, KUORTANE.

### Your Mercy's Cup Has Quenched Our Thirst
Subtitled "Dedication to Service," this text was published in *Sing Glorias for All His Saints* in 1983. Based upon Christ's account of how those redeemed by God have rendered service to "the least of these my brethren," this text is appropriate for a worship service emphasizing social ministry or Christian service.
Suggested tunes: LAKEWOOD, WAREHAM, O HEILIGE DREIFALTIGKEIT.

# PSALM PARAPHRASES

### Psalm 1: How Blest, How Happy Is the Man
Published in *Psalms for the Church Year* (Augsburg, 1975), the psalm was paired with Thomas Tallis's *Sixth Mode Melody*.

Alternate tunes: KINGSFOLD, SARAH-ELIZABETH.

### Psalm 23: The Lord's My Shepherd, See His Grace
Published in *Psalms for the Church Year* (Augsburg, 1975), the psalm was paired with the tune ST. COLUMBA.

### Psalm 90: Our Holy Refuge on This Earth
Published in *Psalms for the Church Year* (Augsburg, 1975), the psalm was paired with Thomas Tallis's *Third Mode Melody*.

Alternate tune: KINGSFOLD.

### Psalm 93: Clothed in Majesty and Light
Published in *Psalms for the Church Year* (Augsburg, 1975), the psalm was paired with the tune TRÖSTET, TRÖSTET SPRICHT DER HERR.

### Psalm 95:1-7: Come, Join the Feast (The *Venite*)
Published in *Psalms for the Church Year* (Augsburg, 1975), this metrical setting of *The Venite* was paired with Thomas Tallis's *First Mode Melody*.

### Psalm 100: All Shades of Men from Dark to Light
Published in *Psalms for the Church Year* (Augsburg, 1975), the metrical stanzas were set to OLD HUNDREDTH (HERR GOTT, DICH LOBEN).

### Psalm 103: He Lets Us See His Treasure
Published in *Psalms for the Church Year* (Augsburg, 1975), the metrical stanzas were set to the tune NUN LOB, MEIN SEEL.

## Psalm 117: Praise Your Creator for the Day

Published in *Psalms for the Church Year* (Augsburg, 1975), the metrical stanzas were set to a German carol tune, in a setting by Carl Schalk.

## Psalm 121: Faithful Father, I Stand Pleading

Published in *Psalms for the Church Year* (Augsburg, 1975), the metrical stanzas were set to *Ainsi qu'on oit le cerf bruine,* by Claude Goudimel.

Alternate tune: FREU DICH SEHR.

# Index of Titles and First Lines

A Mighty Fortress Is Our God (I) .... 27
A Mighty Fortress Is Our God (II) .. 29
A Mighty Fortress Is Our God (III)... 31
A New Song Now Shall Be Begun ... 33
All Glory Be to God Alone ............... 37
All People, Now Make Ready ........... 95
All Shades of Men from
    Dark to Light ............................. 166
All the Nations' Savior, Come ......... 39
Andrew, Hoping for the Kingdom . 125
At Dawn When Came the
    Promised King .......................... 126
'Be Practical,' Our Philip Says ....... 127
Christ Is risen .................................. 96
Christ Jesus to the Jordan Came ...... 41
Christ with Death the Battle Fought ... 43
Clothed in Majesty and Light ......... 164
Come, Holy Ghost,
    God our Friend ............................ 44
Come, Join the Feast ...................... 165
Comfort, Comfort Says the Voice .... 97
Dear Christians, One and All,
    Rejoice ......................................... 45
Dear God, We Offer Thanks
    and Praise ................................. 128
Dear Lord, Your Brother
    Known as James ....................... 129
Enrolled with Christ's Eleven ........ 130

Entrust Your Days and Burdens....... 98
Faithful Father, I Stand Pleading.... 169
From Darkest Canyon
    Depths of Woe ............................ 48
From Heaven Came the
    Angels Bright .............................. 50
From Heaven I Come
    Here Singing Down .................... 51
From Shepherding of Stars ............ 131
Gabriel, You Brought to Mary........ 132
God Blesses Those Who
    Walk His Way ............................. 53
God Brought Me to
    This Time and Place ................. 100
God Holy Ghost, Creator, Come .... 54
God the Father, Be Our Shield ........ 55
God's Own Son
    Conceived in Mary .................... 133
Grant, Holy Ghost,
    That We Behold ........................ 101
Grant, Lord Jesus,
    That My Healing....................... 102
Great God, You Drew
    a Gleaming Earth...................... 134
He Lets Us See His Treasure ........ 167
Here Is the Tenfold Sure
    Command .................................... 57
How Blest, How Happy Is the Man.. 161
If God Were Not Beside Us Now..... 59

| | |
|---|---|
| In Her Arms the Blessed Virgin ..... 135 | *Nunc Dimittis* ................................... 142 |
| In Peace and Joy I Now Depart ....... 60 | O Christ, Our Consolation............. 143 |
| In the Very Midst of Life .................. 61 | O Darkest Woe................................ 114 |
| Isaiah, Mighty Seer, in Spirit Soared ........................... 63 | O Gladsome Light of Grace (*Phos hilaron*) ............................ 144 |
| Jesus Called, 'James, Follow Me Now' ........................ 136 | O God of Heaven, Look Down, Behold............................................ 77 |
| Jesus Christ, Our Blessed Savior ..... 64 | O Jesus, Mighty Conqueror ........... 145 |
| Jesus Christ, Our Mighty King......... 66 | O Light of Light, Your Splendor Bright ........................ 146 |
| Jesus, Shepherd, in Your Arms ....... 104 | O People, Rise and Labor............... 116 |
| Joseph.............................................. 105 | Oh, Grant Us Peace in Our Time, Lord ........................... 79 |
| Let All Together Praise Our God.... 106 | Our Father, Who from Heaven Above .............................. 80 |
| Let Christ Be Glorified as Far .......... 67 | |
| Lift Up Your Heads, You Mighty Gates ............................. 107 | Our Holy Refuge on This Earth..... 163 |
| Look Toward the Mountains ........ 137 | Our Lord Lay Bound in Narrow Room ............................ 82 |
| Lord, for Saint Bartholomew ........ 138 | Physician Luke Delights to Tell........ 147 |
| Lord God, Receive Our Praise and Adoration ............................. 69 | Praise God for John, Evangelist ..... 148 |
| Lord God, We Sing Your Praise........ 70 | Praise God the Holy Spirit ............. 149 |
| Lord, Jesus Christ, We Praise Your Name .................................. 72 | Praise Your Creator for the Day ..... 168 |
| | The Bridegroom Soon Will Call Us.................................. 117 |
| Lord Jesus Christ, Will You Not Stay ...................... 109 | The Bridegroom's Voice Will Soon Be Heard.................... 118 |
| Lord, Keep us Loyal to Your Word .. 73 | The Lord's My Shepherd, See His Grace............................ 162 |
| Lord, When You Came as Welcome Guest........................... 139 | |
| Lord, Your Young Follower, John Mark ................................. 140 | The *Magnificat* ................................ 150 |
| Manger and Word .......................... 110 | The Unwise Tongue of Man May Say........................................ 84 |
| Mary Went Up to Hill Country ...... 141 | The Very Skies Served You, O Lord ........................................ 151 |
| May God Takee Us into His Grace .................................... 74 | |
| My Bride, the Church, Is Dear to Me............................... 75 | Thy Planting .................................... 152 |
| | To Us a Little Child Is Born............ 119 |
| Now Let Us Come Before Him...... 112 | To You We Pray, the Holy Ghost ..... 86 |
| Now Sing We, Now Rejoice............ 113 | True God from All Eternity.............. 87 |

Unite Your Voices,
   Praise Our God............................ 120
We All Believe in One True God ...... 88
We Praise, O Christ,
   Your Holy Name .......................... 89
We Praise You, God the Father ....... 153
We Praise Your Call to Matthew .... 154
When Christ Went Where
   He Would Be Slain ..................... 155

When I Suffer Pains and Losses..... 121
Why Would Foe Herod
   and His Horde .............................. 90
You Planted Us in Sun and Rain ... 156
You Want to Live Your Life Aright ... 91
Your Jude and Zealot Simon ......... 157
Your Mercy's Cup Has
   Quenched Our Thirst ................ 158

www.ingramcontent.com/pod-product-compliance
Lightning Source LLC
Chambersburg PA
CBHW050317120526
**44592CB00014B/1952**